Angle Classification and Measurement

6th Grade Geometry Books

Vol II

Children's Math Books

Speedy Publishing LLC
40 E. Main St. #1156
Newark, DE 19711
www.speedypublishing.com

Angle Measurement

NAME: ______________________________

EXERCISE 1

Measure the Angle to the Nearest Degree.

1)

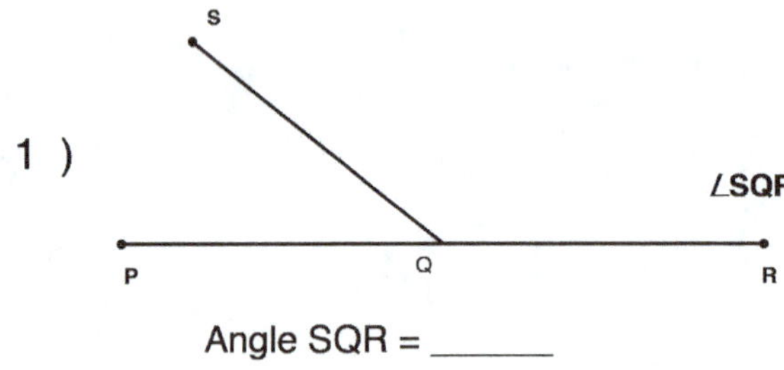

Angle SQR = ______

2)

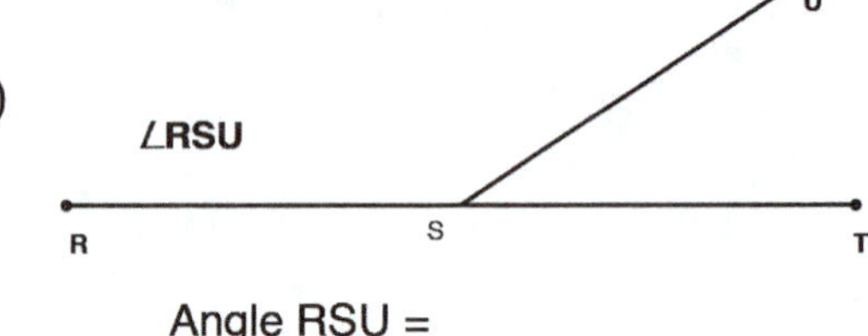

Angle RSU = ______

3)

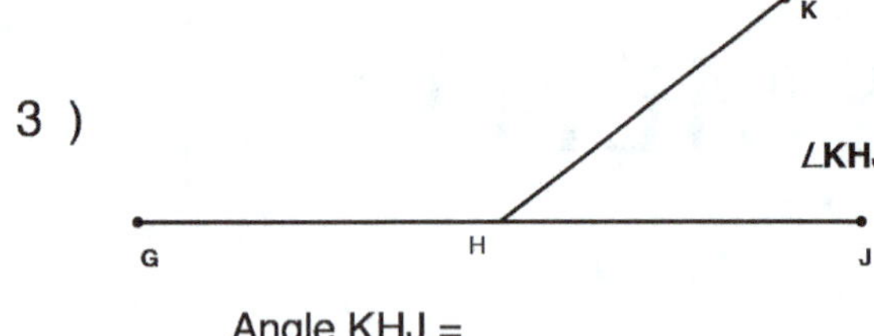

Angle KHJ = ______

4)

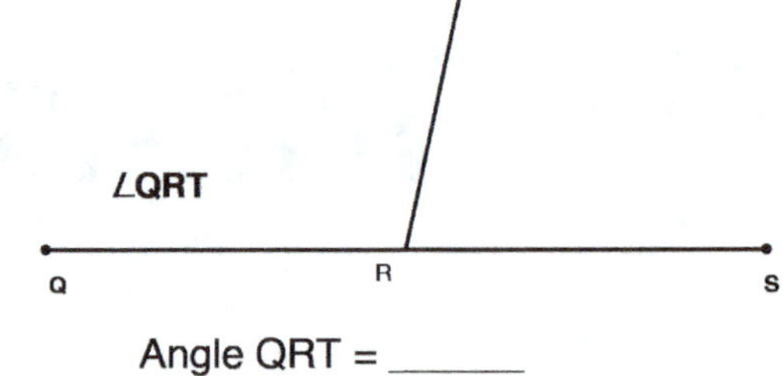

Angle QRT = ______

5)

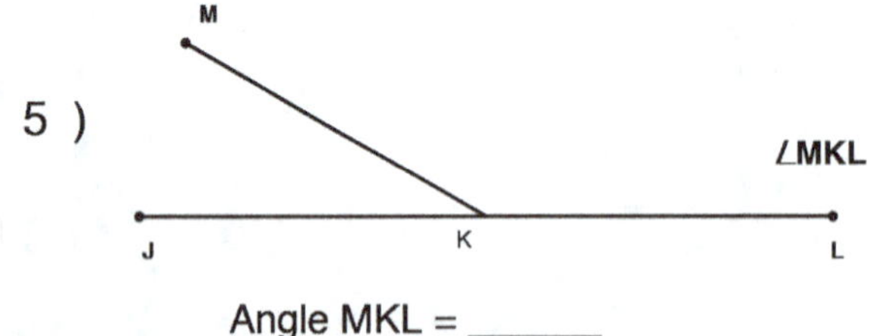

Angle MKL = ______

6)

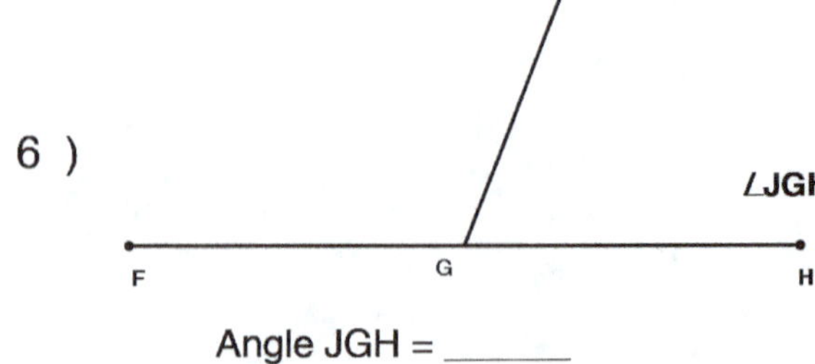

Angle JGH = ______

NAME: ______________________________

EXERCISE 2

Measure the Angle to the Nearest Degree.

1)

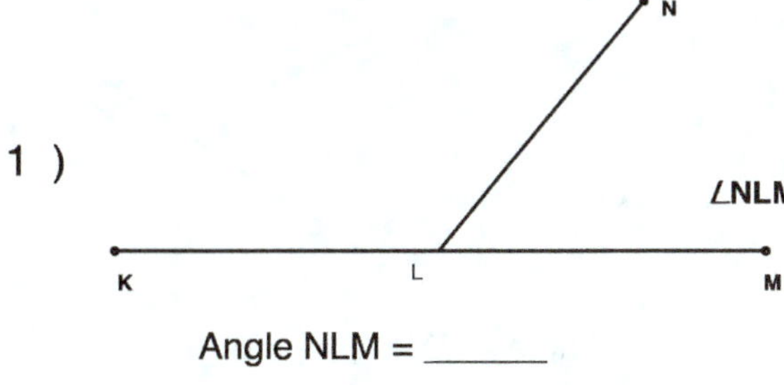

Angle NLM = ______

2)

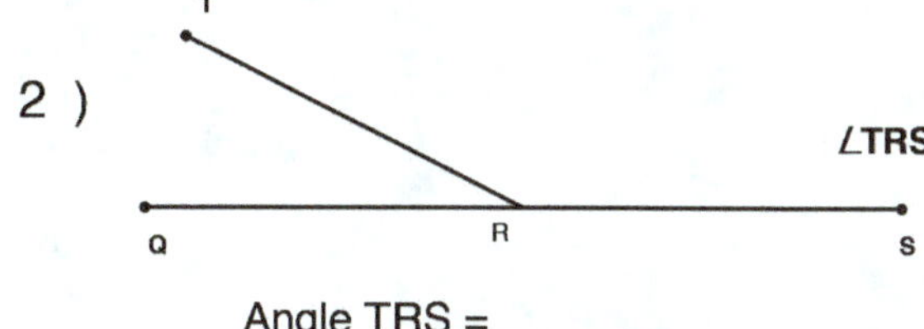

Angle TRS = ______

3)

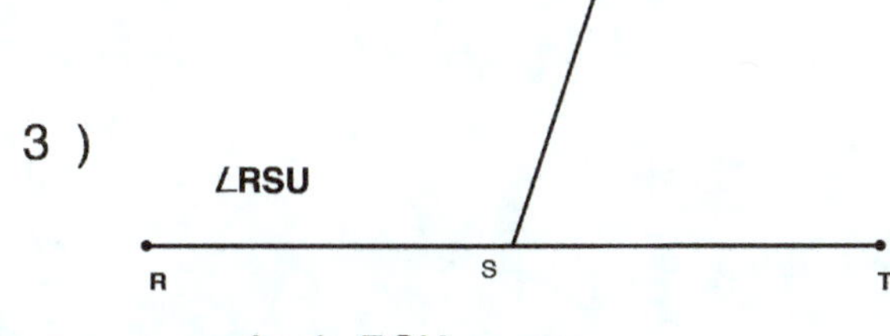

Angle RSU = ______

4)

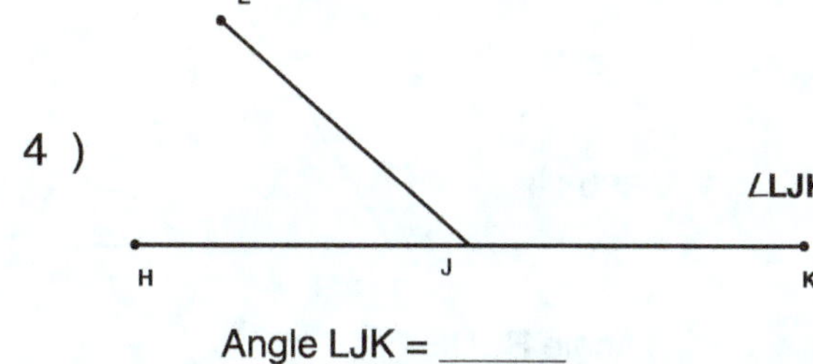

Angle LJK = ______

5)

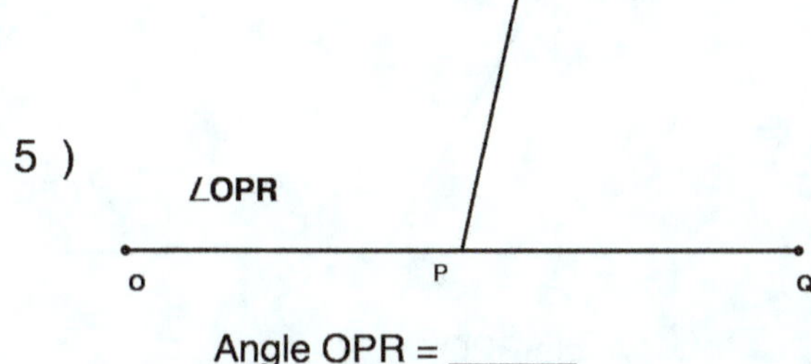

Angle OPR = ______

6)

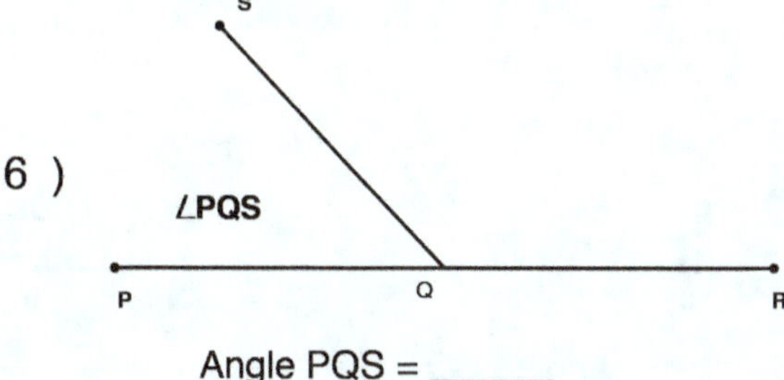

Angle PQS = ______

NAME: ______________________________

EXERCISE 3

Measure the Angle to the Nearest Degree.

1)

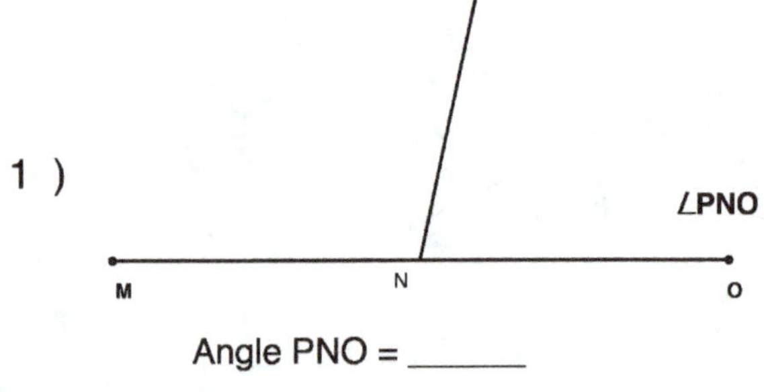

Angle PNO = ______

2)

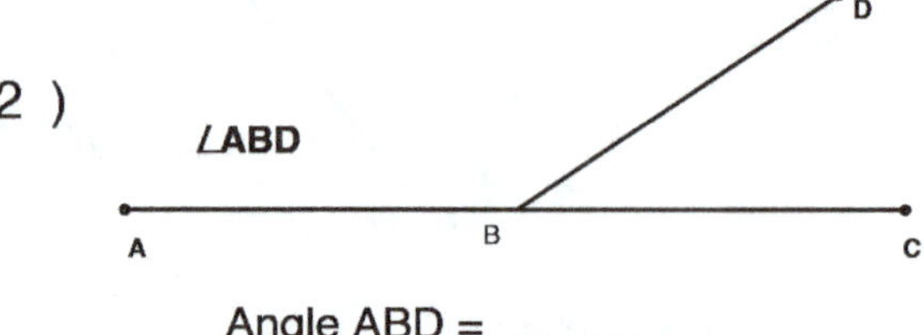

Angle ABD = ______

3)

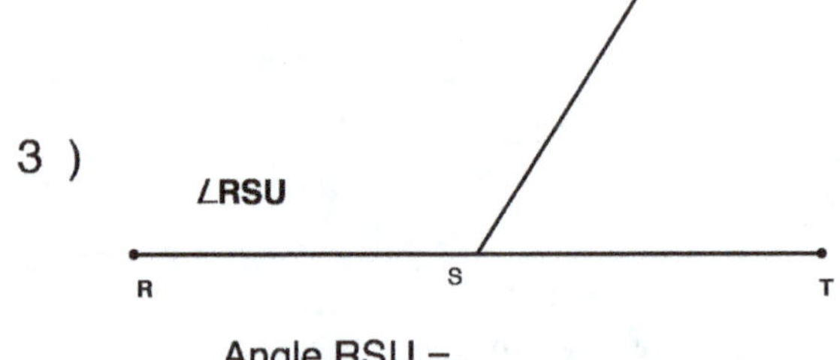

Angle RSU = ______

4)

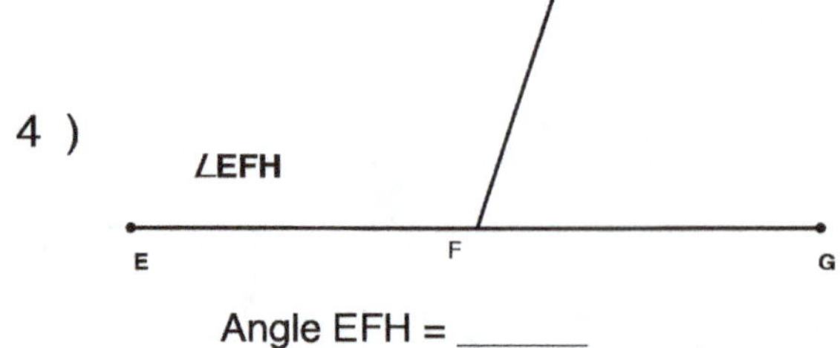

Angle EFH = ______

5)

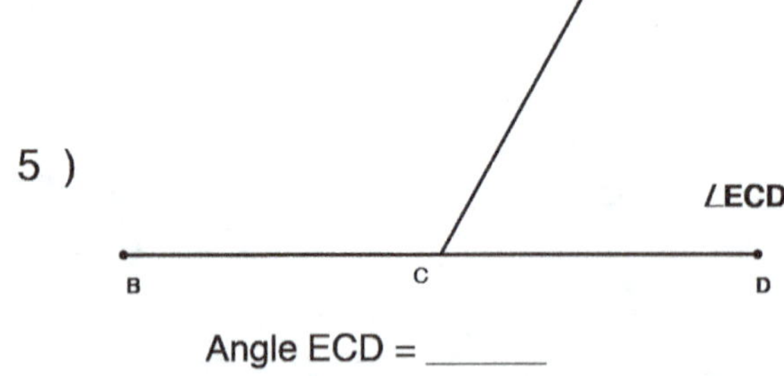

Angle ECD = ______

6)

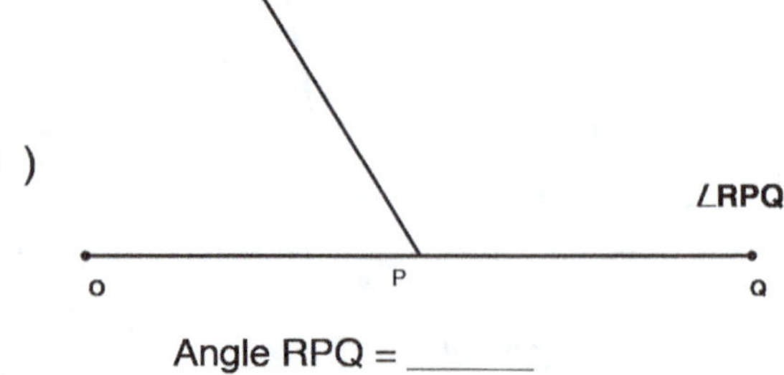

Angle RPQ = ______

NAME: ______________________________

EXERCISE 4

Measure the Angle to the Nearest Degree.

1)

∠JGH

F G H

Angle JGH = ______

2)

E

∠BCE

B C D

Angle BCE = ______

3)

R

∠RPQ

O P Q

Angle RPQ = ______

4)

T

∠QRT

Q R S

Angle QRT = ______

5)

S

∠PQS

P Q R

Angle PQS = ______

6)

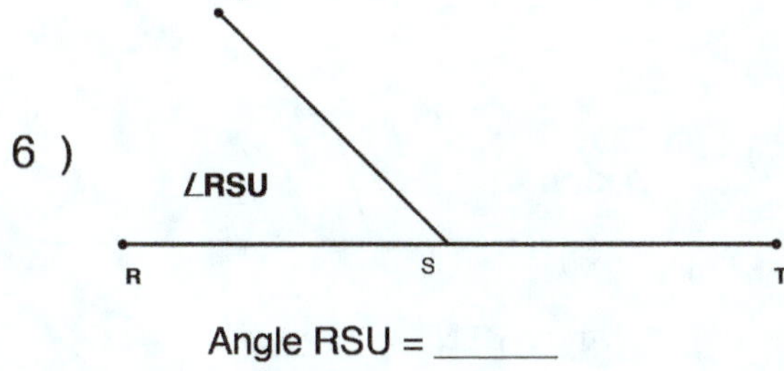

Angle RSU = ______

NAME: ______________________________

EXERCISE
5

Measure the Angle to the Nearest Degree.

1)

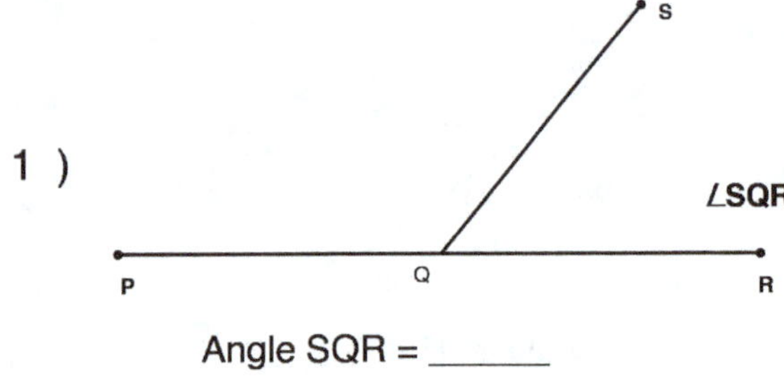

Angle SQR = ______

2)

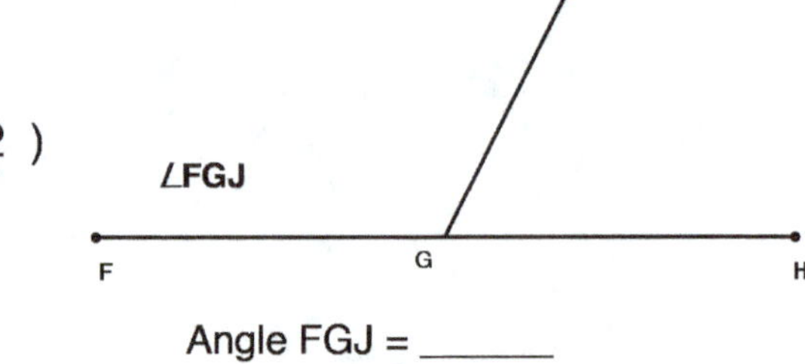

Angle FGJ = ______

3)

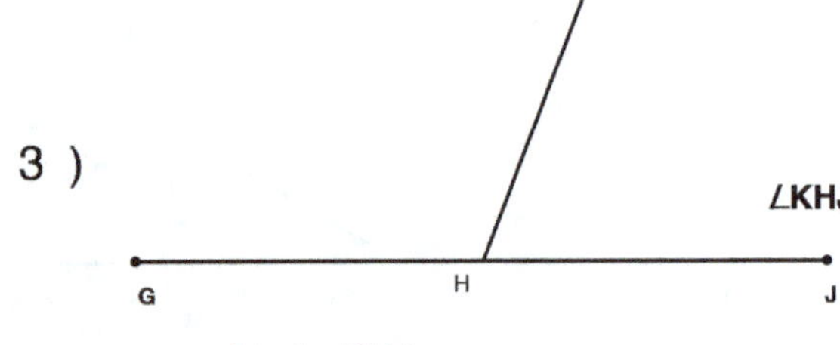

Angle KHJ = ______

4)

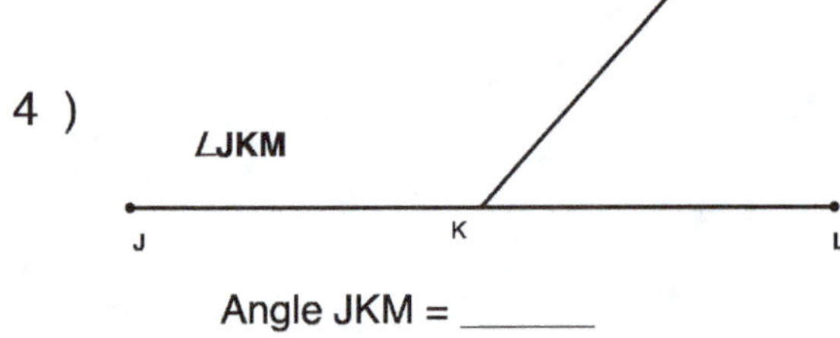

Angle JKM = ______

5)

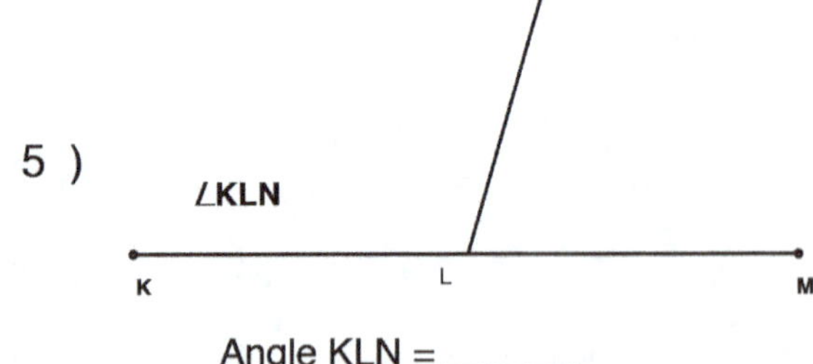

Angle KLN = ______

6)

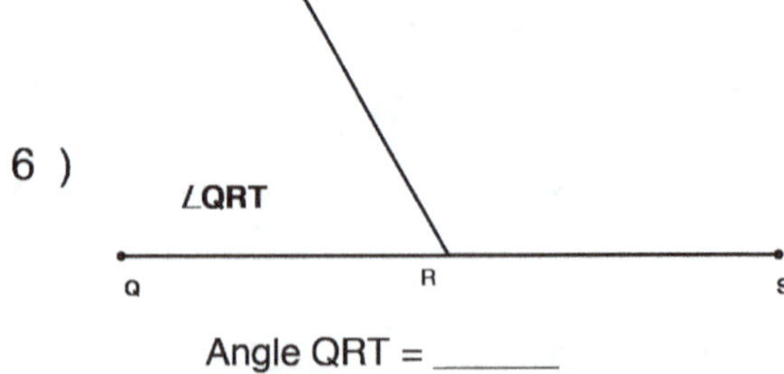

Angle QRT = ______

NAME: ______________________________

EXERCISE 6

Measure the Angle to the Nearest Degree.

1)

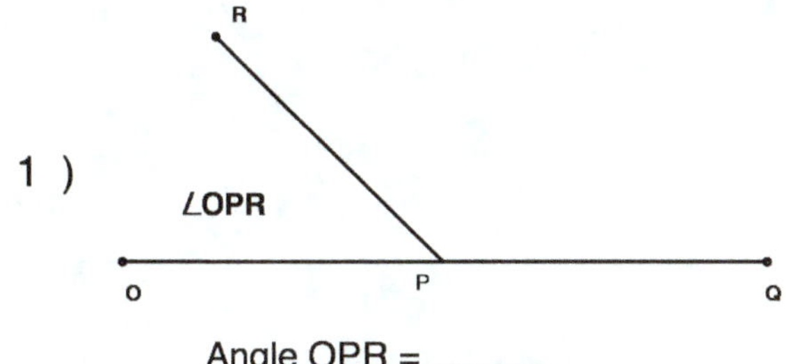

Angle OPR = ______

2)

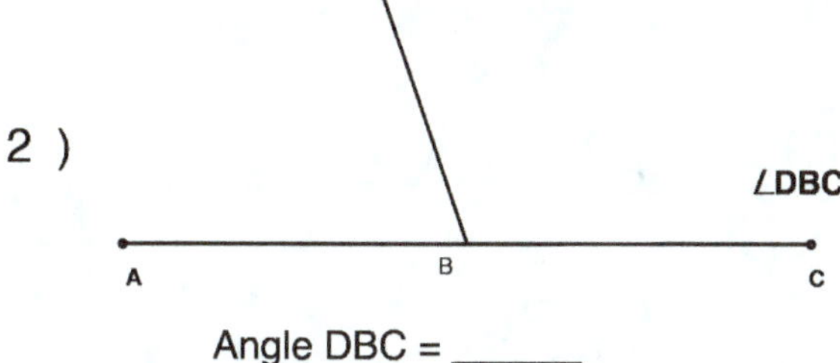

Angle DBC = ______

3)

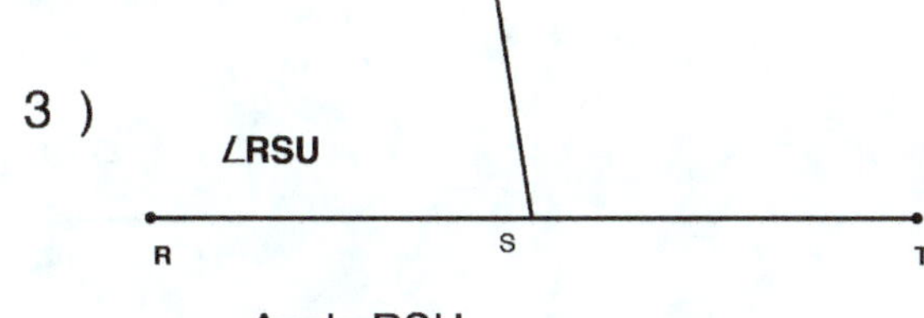

Angle RSU = ______

4)

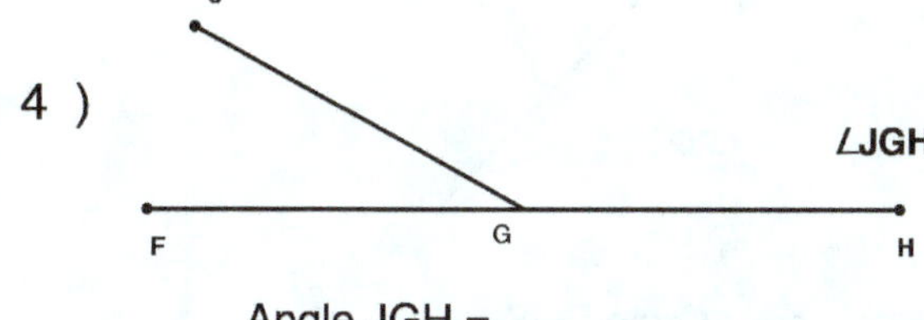

Angle JGH = ______

5)

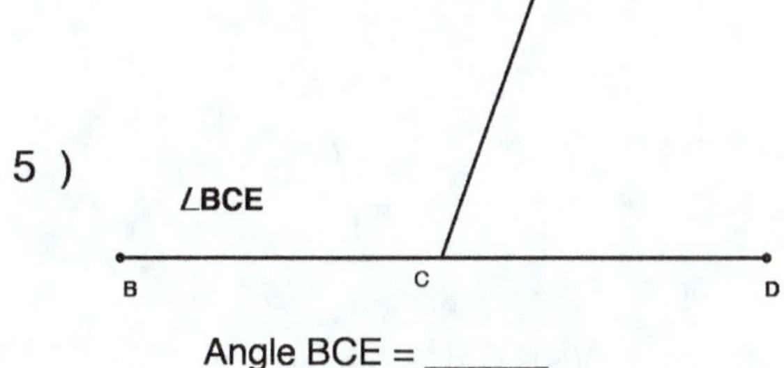

Angle BCE = ______

6)

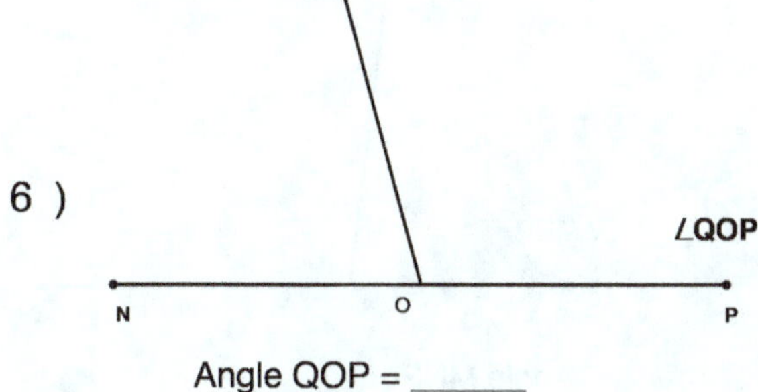

Angle QOP = ______

NAME: ______________________________

EXERCISE 7

Measure the Angle to the Nearest Degree.

1)

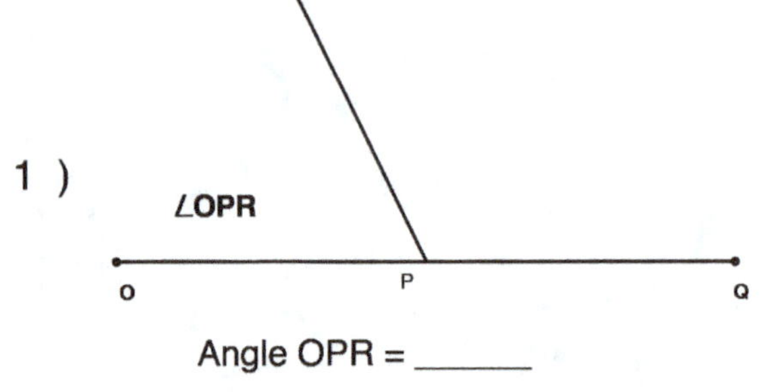

Angle OPR = ______

2)

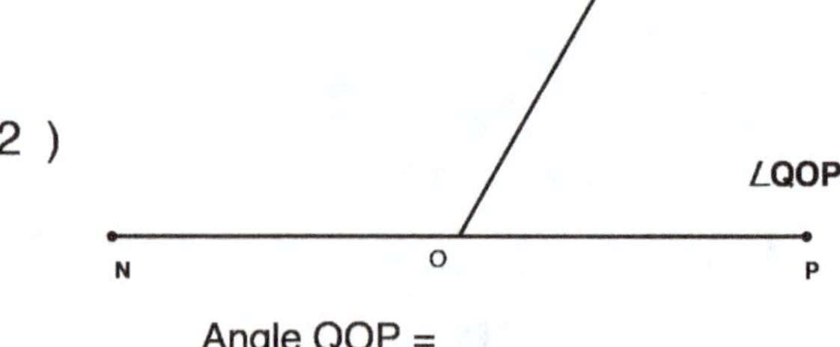

Angle QOP = ______

3)

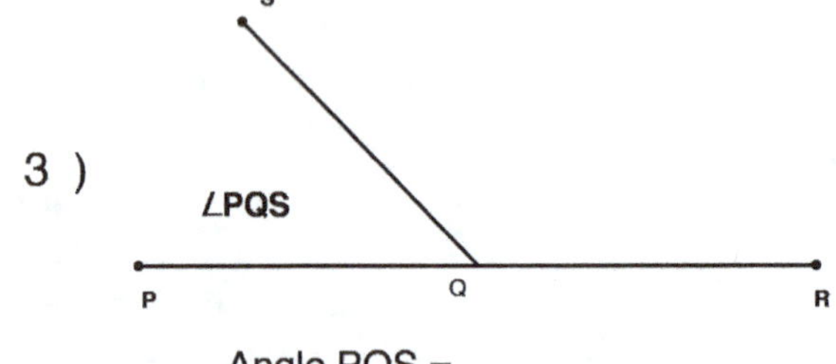

Angle PQS = ______

4)

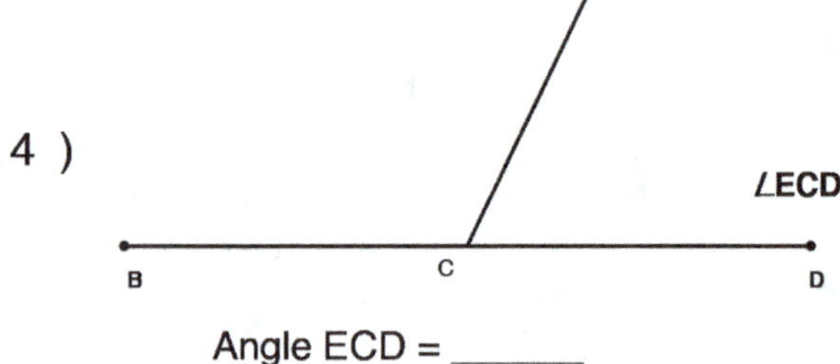

Angle ECD = ______

5)

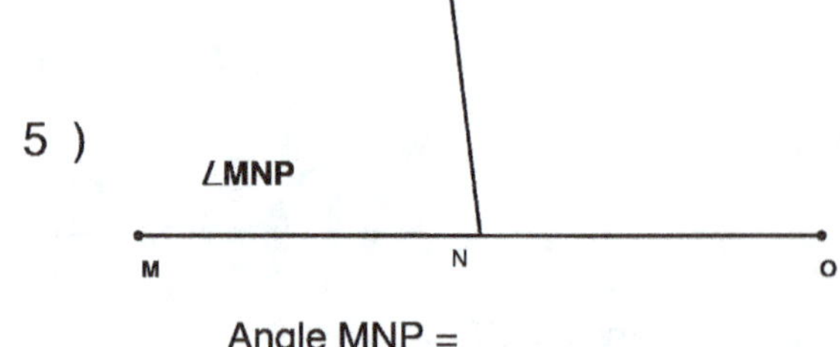

Angle MNP = ______

6)

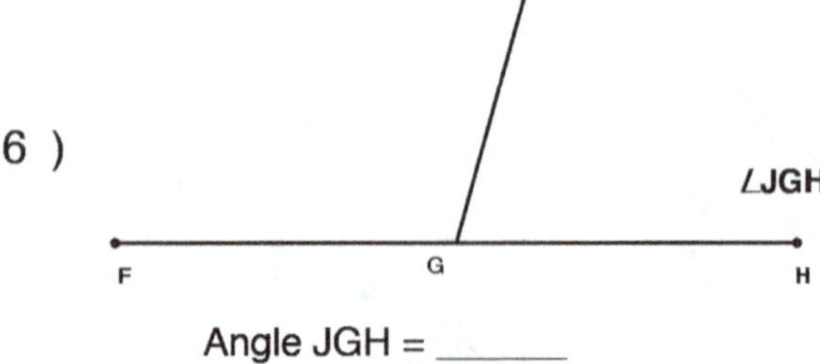

Angle JGH = ______

NAME: ______________________________

EXERCISE 8

Measure the Angle to the Nearest Degree.

1)

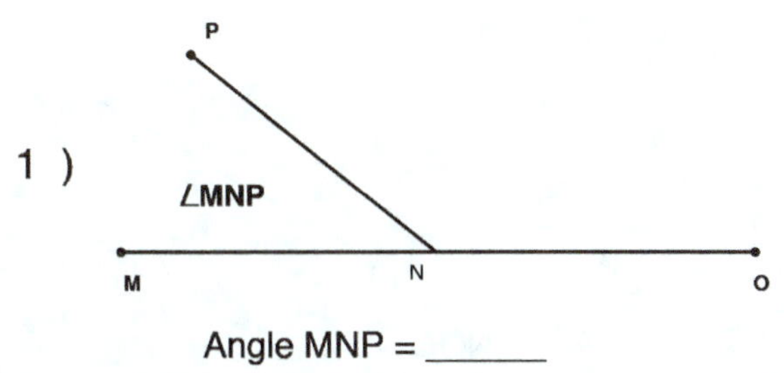

Angle MNP = ______

2)

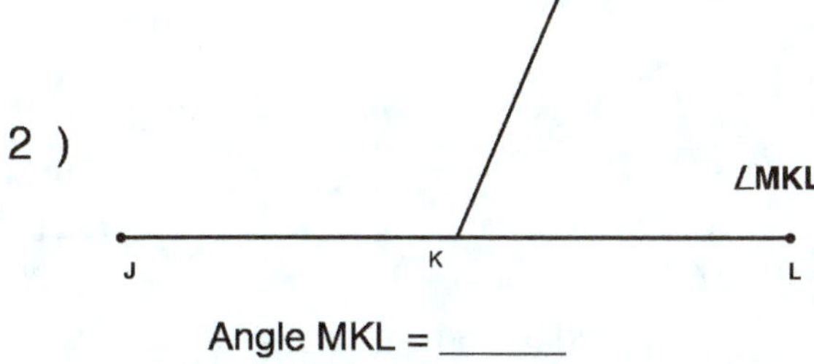

Angle MKL = ______

3)

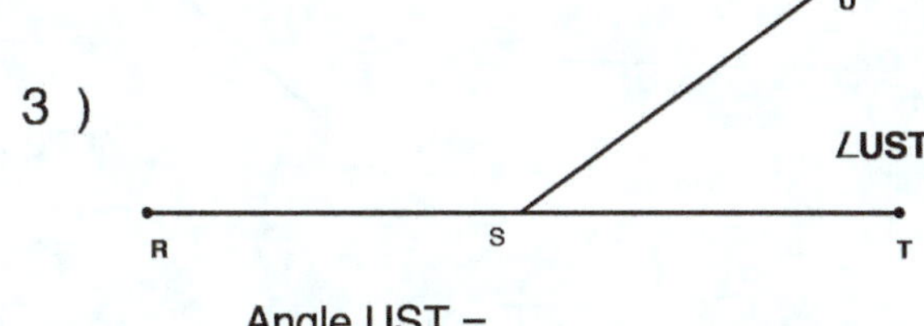

Angle UST = ______

4)

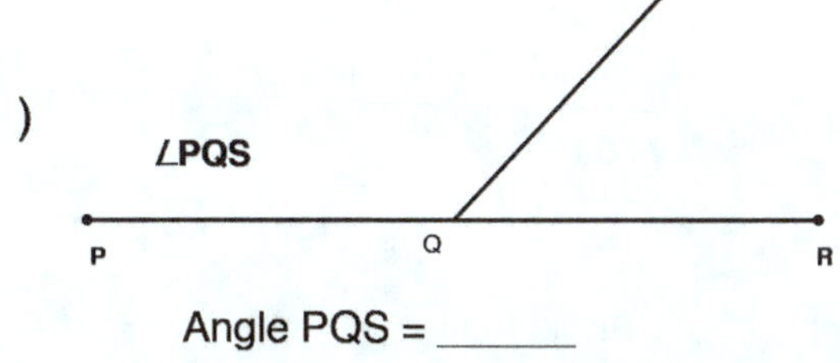

Angle PQS = ______

5)

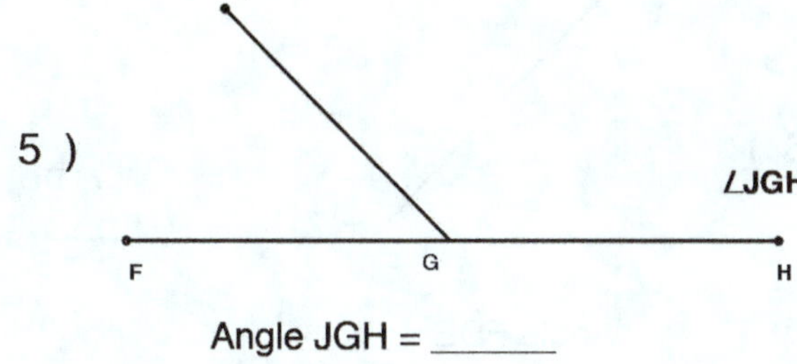

Angle JGH = ______

6)

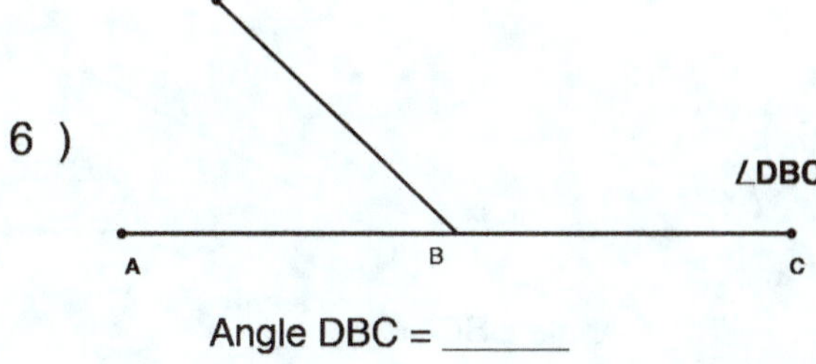

Angle DBC = ______

NAME: ______________________________

EXERCISE 9

Measure the Angle to the Nearest Degree.

1)

N

∠NLM

K L M

Angle NLM = ______

2)

Q

∠NOQ

N O P

Angle NOQ = ______

3)

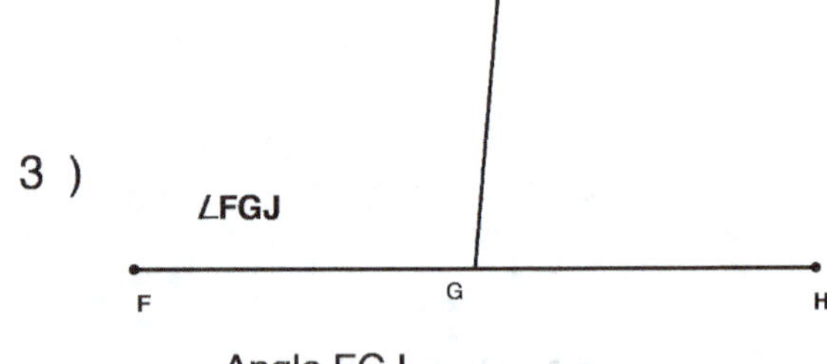

Angle FGJ = ______

4)

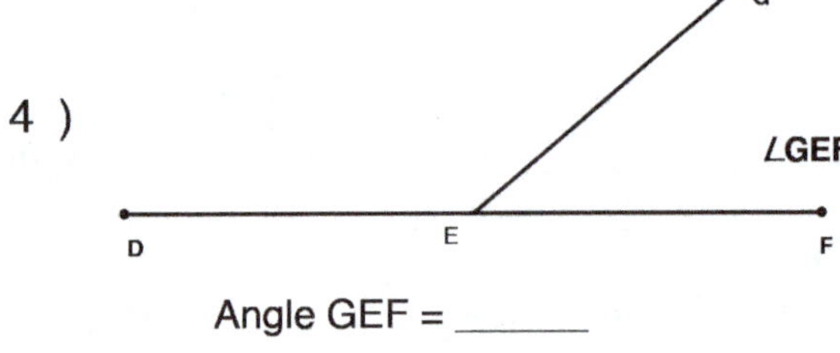

Angle GEF = ______

5)

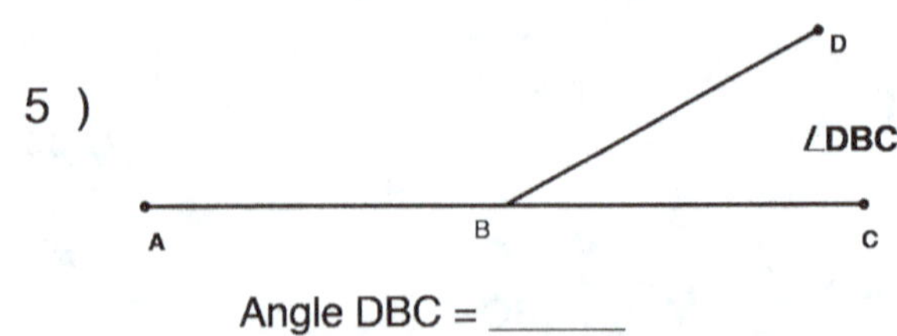

Angle DBC = ______

6)

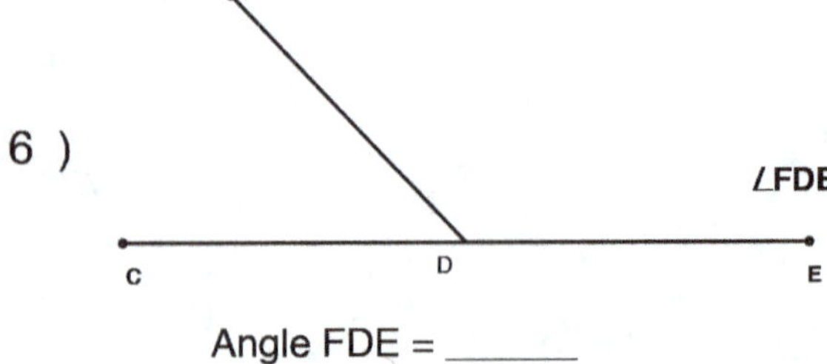

Angle FDE = ______

NAME: ______________________

EXERCISE 10

Measure the Angle to the Nearest Degree.

1) ∠SQR

S, P, Q, R

Angle SQR = ______

2) ∠NOQ

Q, N, O, P

Angle NOQ = ______

3) ∠TRS

T, Q, R, S

Angle TRS = ______

4) ∠KLN

N, K, L, M

Angle KLN = ______

5) ∠ECD

E, B, C, D

Angle ECD = ______

6)

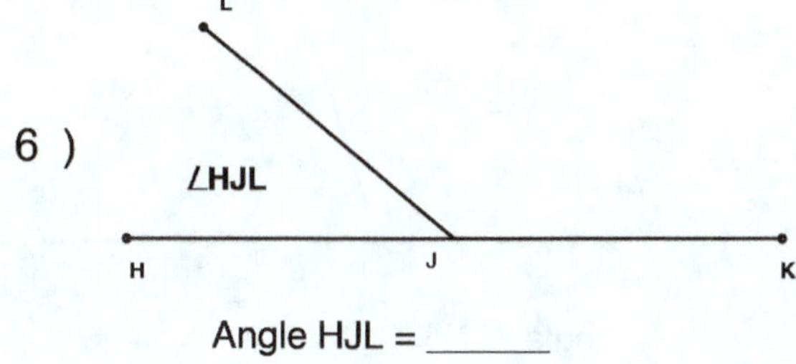

Angle HJL = ______

NAME: ___________________

EXERCISE 11

Measure the Angle to the Nearest Degree.

1) 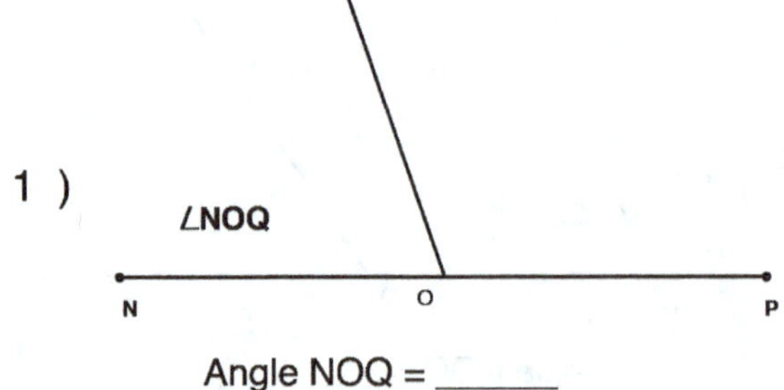

Angle NOQ = ______

2) 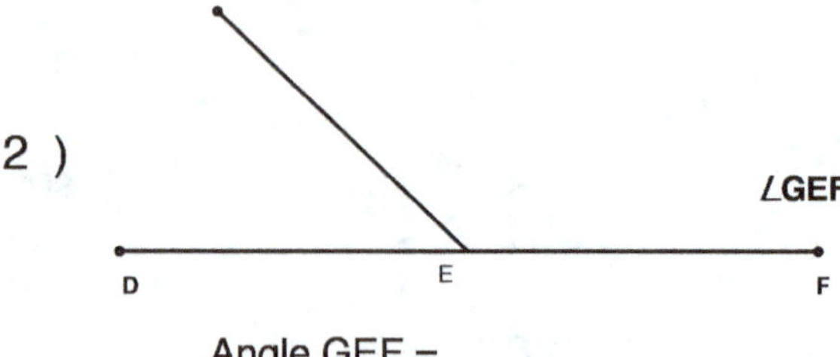

Angle GEF = ______

3) 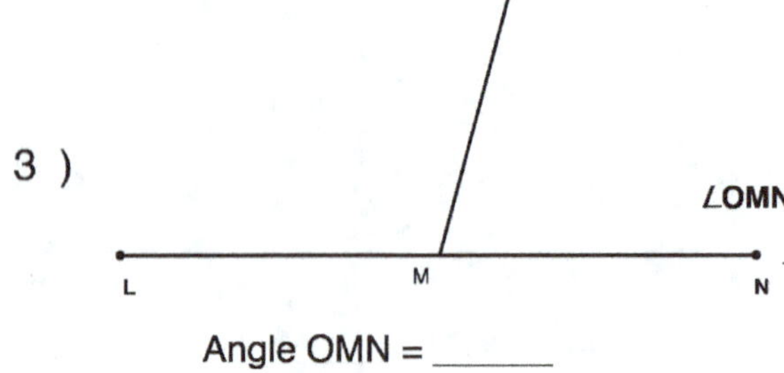

Angle OMN = ______

4) 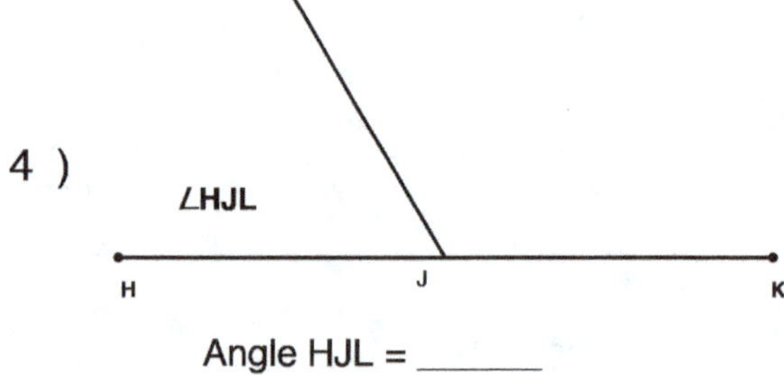

Angle HJL = ______

5) 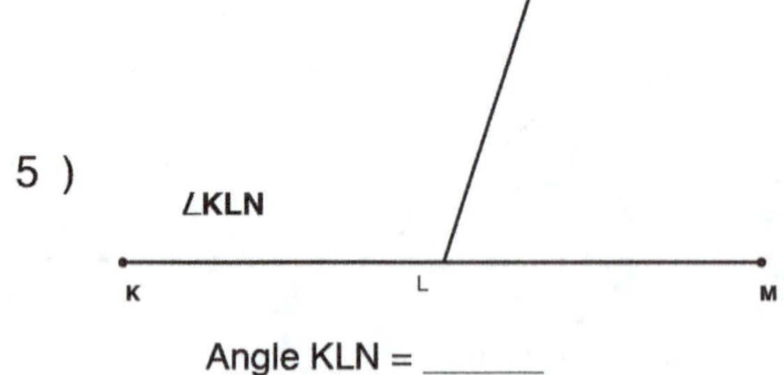

Angle KLN = ______

6) 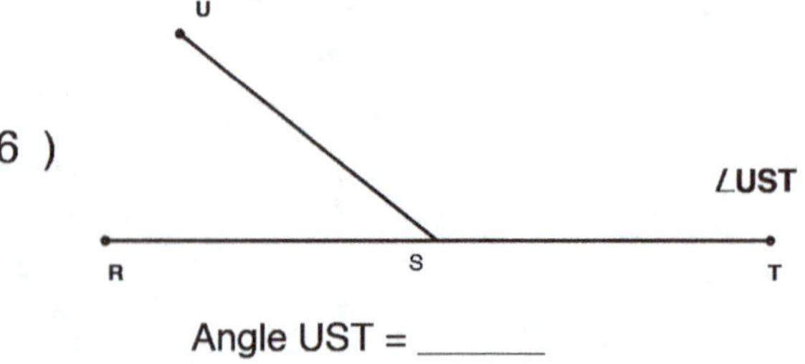

Angle UST = ______

NAME: ____________________

EXERCISE 12

Measure the Angle to the Nearest Degree.

1) ∠RSU

Angle RSU = ______

2) ∠HJL

Angle HJL = ______

3) ∠MKL

Angle MKL = ______

4) ∠BCE

Angle BCE = ______

5) ∠GEF

Angle GEF = ______

6) ∠ABD

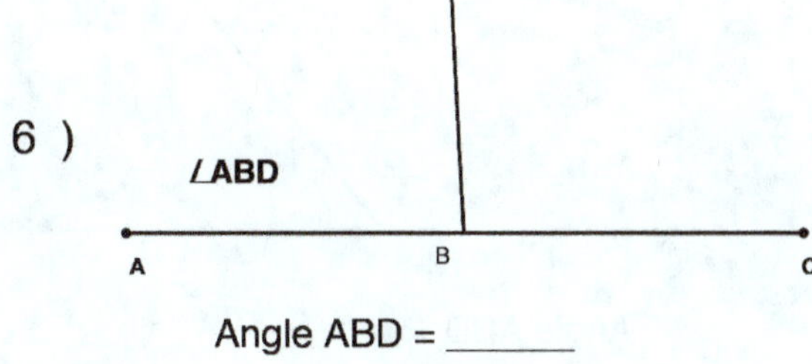

Angle ABD = ______

NAME: ______________________________

EXERCISE 13

Measure the Angle to the Nearest Degree.

1) ∠FDE

F, C, D, E

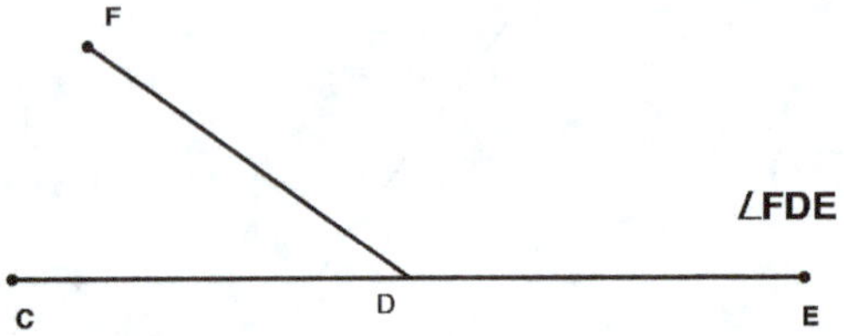

Angle FDE = ______

2) ∠MKL

M, J, K, L

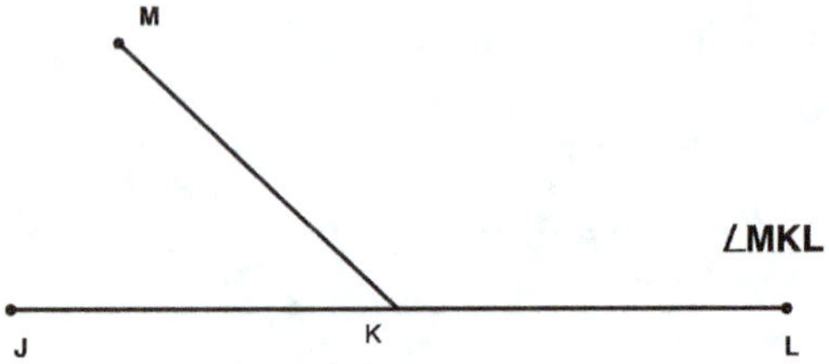

Angle MKL = ______

3) ∠QOP

Q, N, O, P

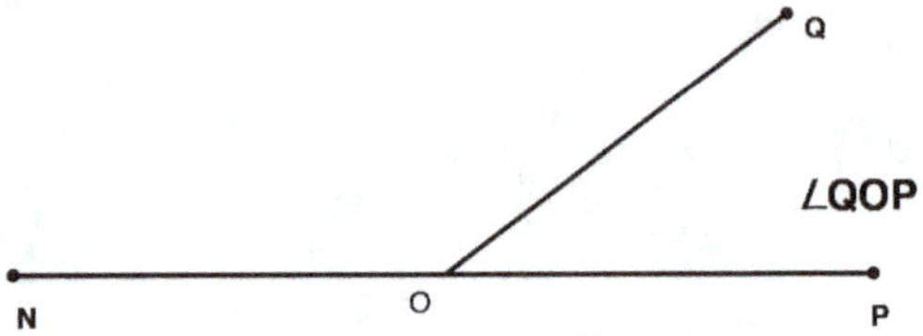

Angle QOP = ______

4) ∠PQS

S, P, Q, R

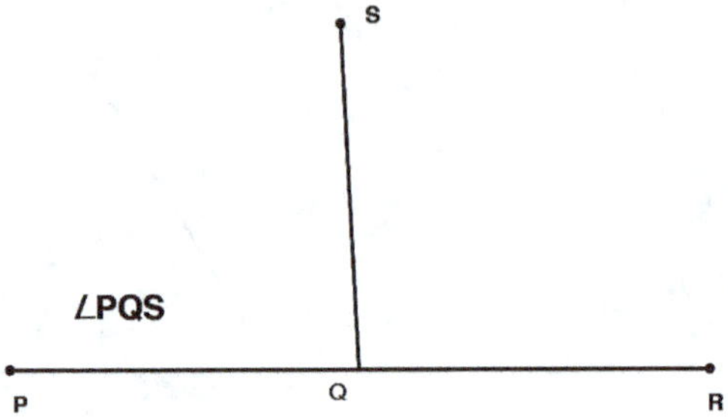

Angle PQS = ______

5) ∠ABD

D, A, B, C

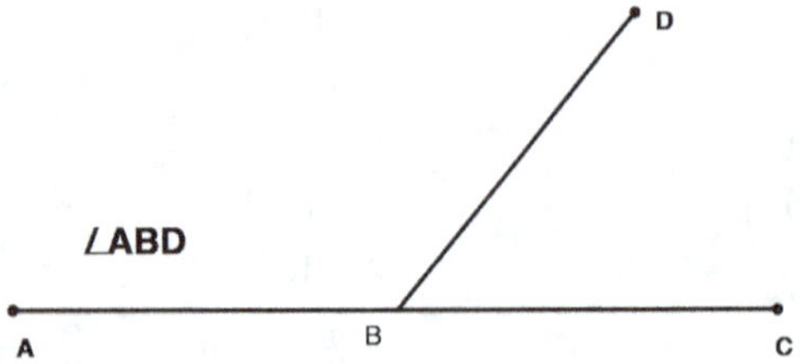

Angle ABD = ______

6) ∠GHK

K, G, H, J

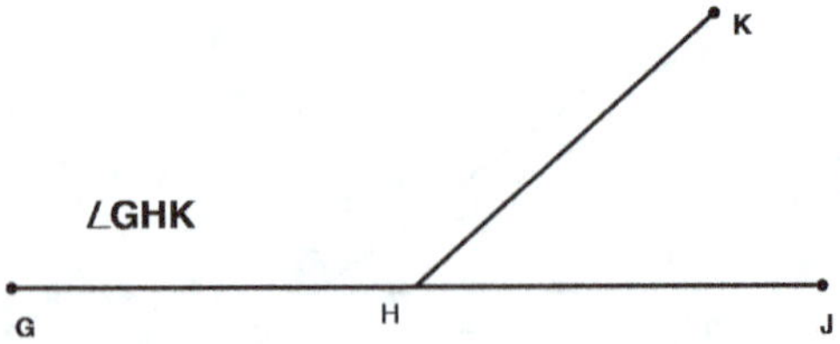

Angle GHK = ______

NAME: ______________________________

Measure the Angle to the Nearest Degree.

EXERCISE 14

1)

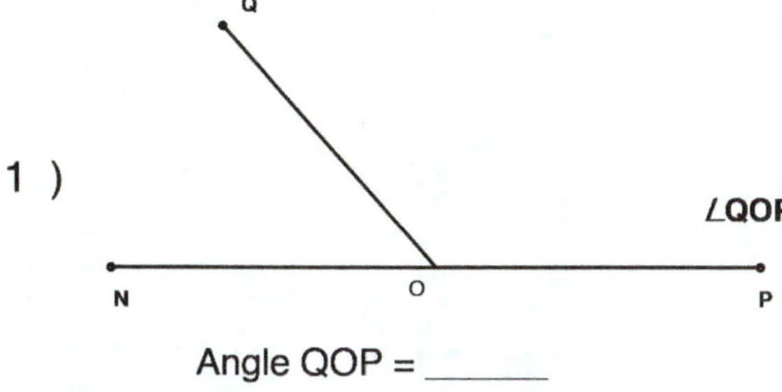

Angle QOP = ______

2)

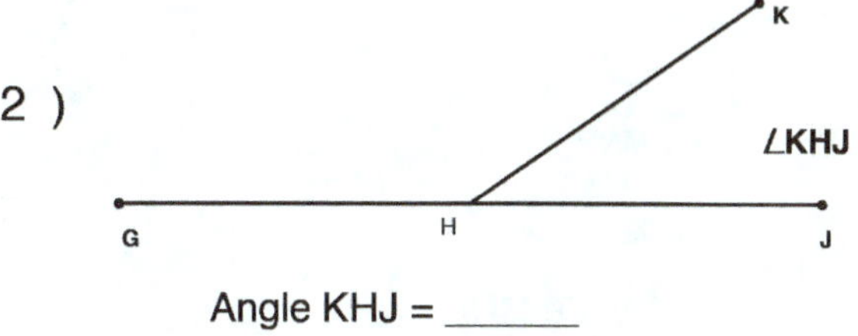

Angle KHJ = ______

3)

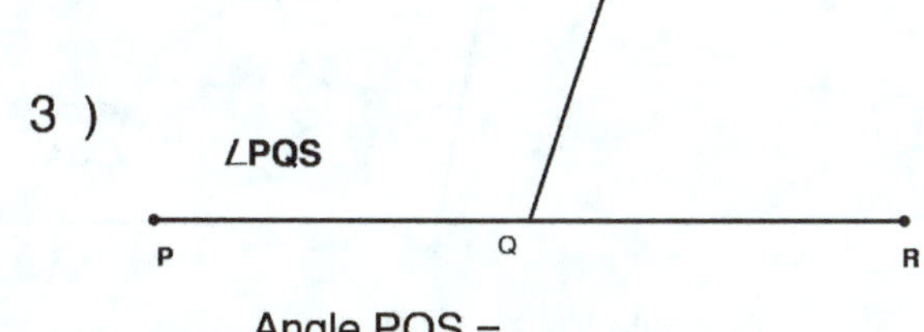

Angle PQS = ______

4)

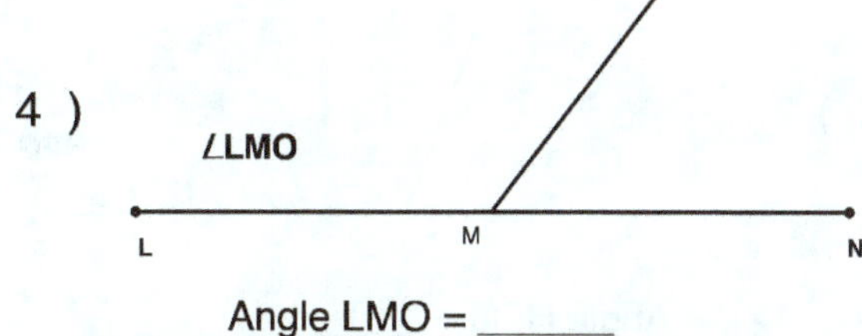

Angle LMO = ______

5)

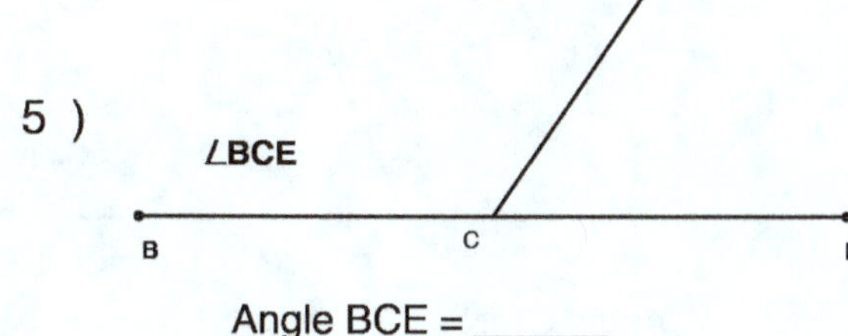

Angle BCE = ______

6)

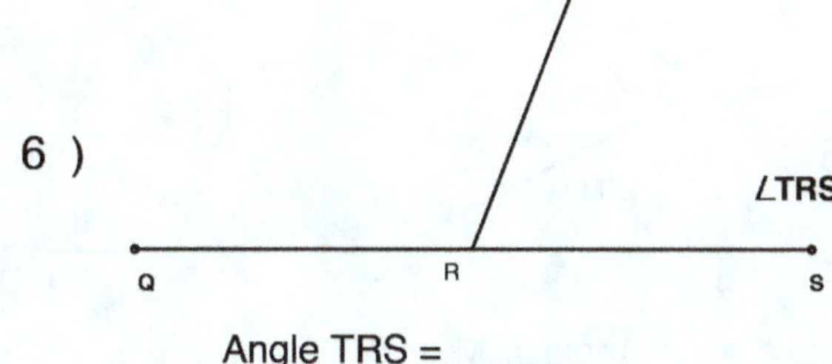

Angle TRS = ______

NAME: ________________________________

EXERCISE 15

Measure the Angle to the Nearest Degree.

1)

∠MNP

M N O

Angle MNP = ______

2)

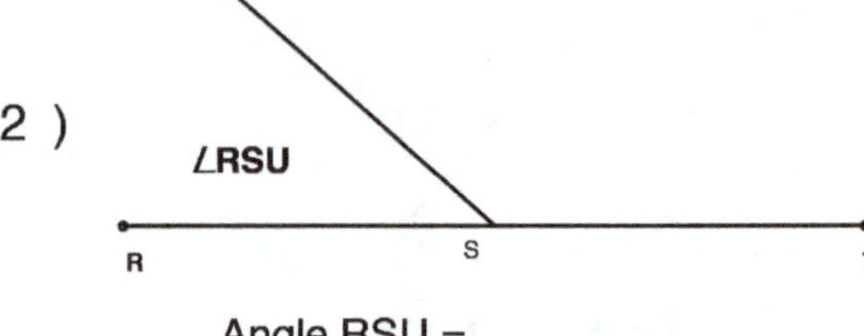

Angle RSU = ______

3)

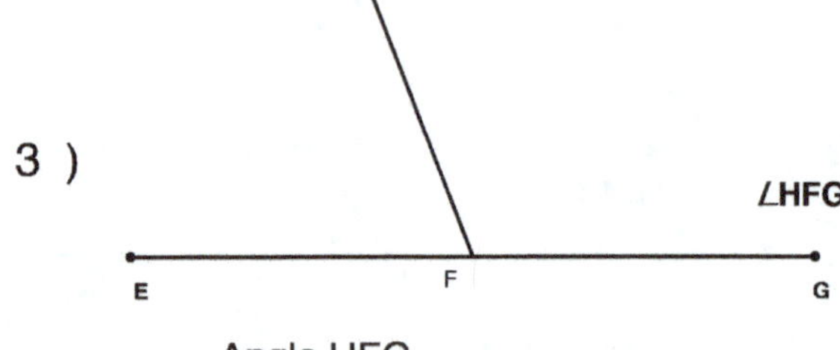

Angle HFG = ______

4)

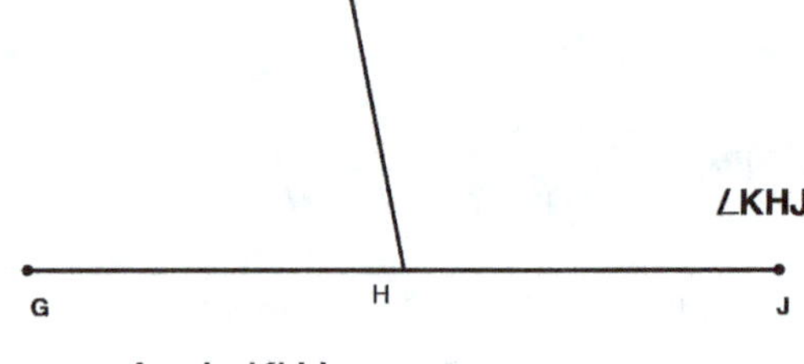

Angle KHJ = ______

5)

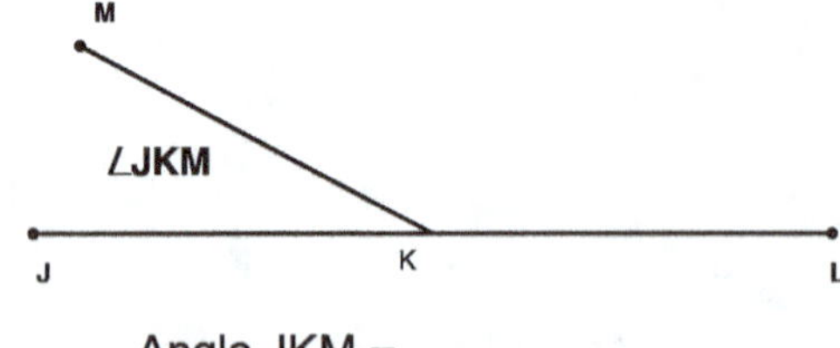

Angle JKM = ______

6)

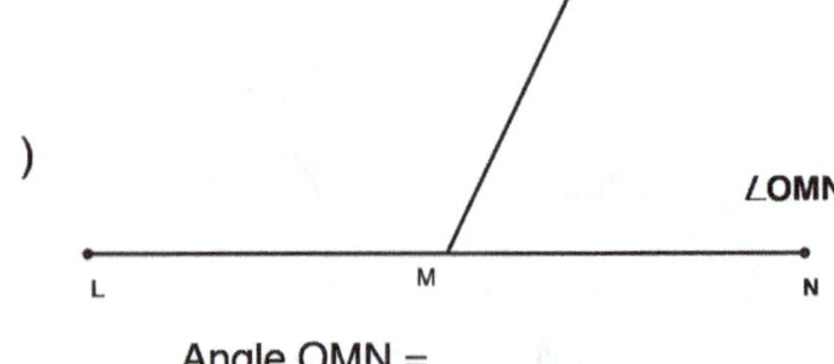

Angle OMN = ______

Angle Classification

NAME: ______________________

Classify each angle as acute, obtuse, right, or straight.

1)  __________

2)  __________

3)  __________

4)  __________

5)  __________

EXERCISE 1

NAME: ______________________________

Classify each angle as acute, obtuse, right, or straight.

6)  ____________

7)  ____________

8)  ____________

9) ____________

10) ____________

NAME: ______________________________

Classify each angle as acute, obtuse, right, or straight.

1)  ____________

2)  ____________

3)  ____________

4)  ____________

5)  ____________

EXERCISE 2

NAME: ______________________________

Classify each angle as acute, obtuse, right, or straight.

6)  ____________

7) ____________

8) ____________

9) ____________

10) ____________

NAME: ______________________________

Classify each angle as acute, obtuse, right, or straight.

1)  ____________

2)  ____________

3)  ____________

4)  ____________

5)  ____________

EXERCISE 3

NAME: ______________________________

Classify each angle as acute, obtuse, right, or straight.

6)  __________

7)  __________

8)  __________

9)  __________

10)  __________

NAME: ______________________

Classify each angle as acute, obtuse, right, or straight.

1) ____________

2) ____________

3) ____________

4) ____________

5) ____________

EXERCISE 4

NAME: ______________________________

Classify each angle as acute, obtuse, right, or straight.

6) ____________

7) ____________

8) ____________

9) ____________

10) ____________

NAME: ____________________

Classify each angle as acute, obtuse, right, or straight.

1) ____________

2) ____________

3) ____________

4) ____________

5) ____________

EXERCISE 5

NAME: ______________________________

Classify each angle as acute, obtuse, right, or straight.

6) ______________

7) ______________

8) ______________

9) ______________

10) ______________

NAME: ______________________________

Classify each angle as acute, obtuse, right, or straight.

1)  ____________

2)  ____________

3)  ____________

4)  ____________

5)  ____________

EXERCISE 6

NAME: ______________________________

Classify each angle as acute, obtuse, right, or straight.

6)  ____________

7)  ____________

8)  ____________

9) ____________

10) ____________

NAME: ______________________________

Classify each angle as acute, obtuse, right, or straight.

1) 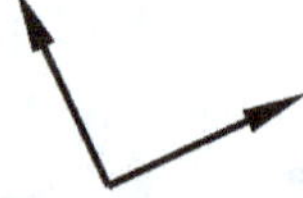 ____________

2)  ____________

3)  ____________

4)  ____________

5)  ____________

EXERCISE 7

NAME: ______________________________

Classify each angle as acute, obtuse, right, or straight.

6)  ____________

7) ____________

8) ____________

9) ____________

10) ____________

NAME: ___________________________

Classify each angle as acute, obtuse, right, or straight.

1)  ____________

2)  ____________

3)  ____________

4)  ____________

5)  ____________

EXERCISE 8

NAME: ______________________

Classify each angle as acute, obtuse, right, or straight.

6)  __________

7)  __________

8)  __________

9) __________

10) __________

NAME: ______________________________

Classify each angle as acute, obtuse, right, or straight.

1) 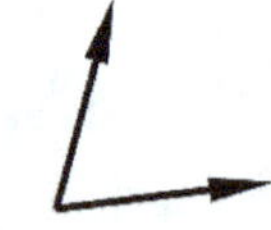 ______________

2)  ______________

3)  ______________

4)  ______________

5)  ______________

EXERCISE 9

NAME: ______________________________

Classify each angle as acute, obtuse, right, or straight.

6)

7) ____________

8) ____________

9) ____________

10) ____________

NAME: ______________________________

Classify each angle as acute, obtuse, right, or straight.

1) ____________

2) ____________

3) ____________

4) ____________

5) ____________

EXERCISE 10

NAME: ______________________________

Classify each angle as acute, obtuse, right, or straight.

6) ____________

7) ____________

8) ____________

9) ____________

10) ____________

Angle Classification

NAME: ______________________________

Classify each angle as acute, obtuse, right, or straight.

1. 143° = ____________

2. 111° = ____________

3. 10° = ____________

4. 102° = ____________

5. 74° = ____________

6. 124° = ____________

7. 116° = ____________

8. 126° = ____________

9. 158° = ____________

10. 39° = ____________

11. 77° = ____________

12. 31° = ____________

13. 133° = ____________

14. 113° = ____________

15. 34° = ____________

16. 127° = ____________

17. 139° = ____________

18. 174° = ____________

19. 84° = ____________

20. 165° = ____________

Answers

ANGLE MEASUREMENT

EXERCISE 1

1) ∠SQR

S, P, Q, R

Angle SQR = 141°

2) ∠RSU

U, R, S, T

Angle RSU = 146°

3) ∠KHJ

K, G, H, J

Angle KHJ = 38°

4) ∠QRT

T, Q, R, S

Angle QRT = 102°

5) ∠MKL

M, J, K, L

Angle MKL = 150°

6) ∠JGH

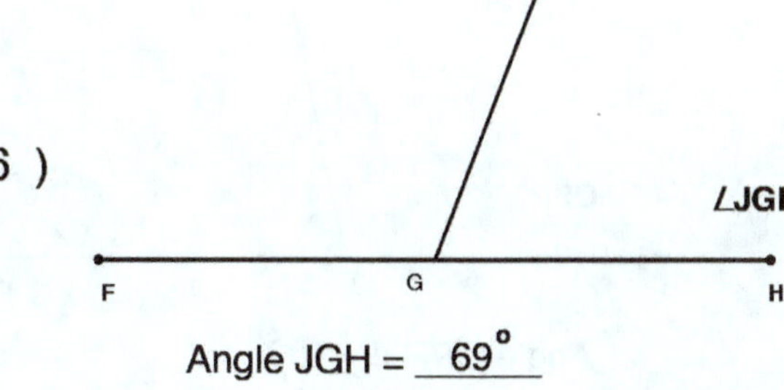

Angle JGH = 69°

EXERCISE 2

1)

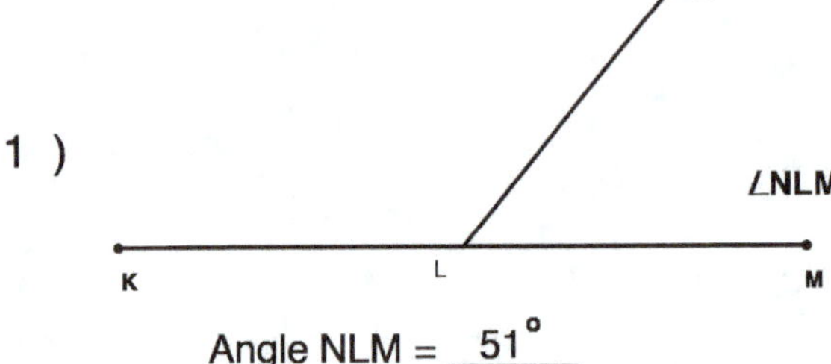

Angle NLM = 51°

2)

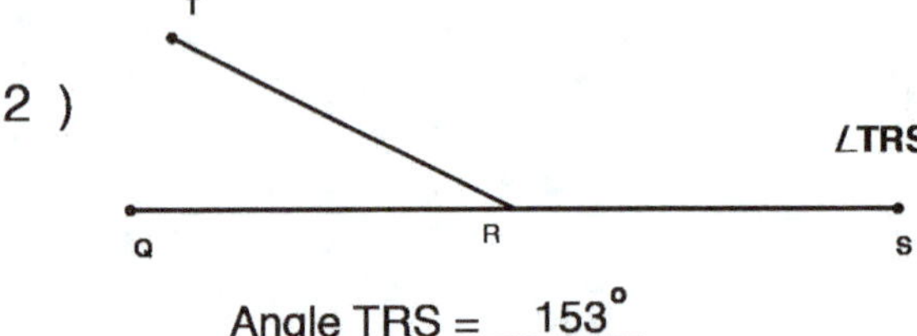

Angle TRS = 153°

3)

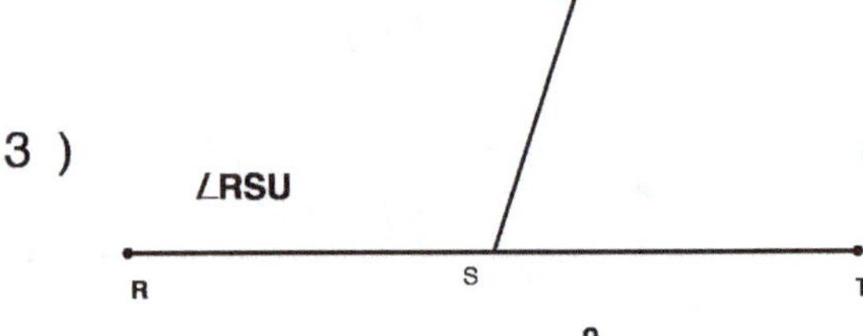

Angle RSU = 108°

4)

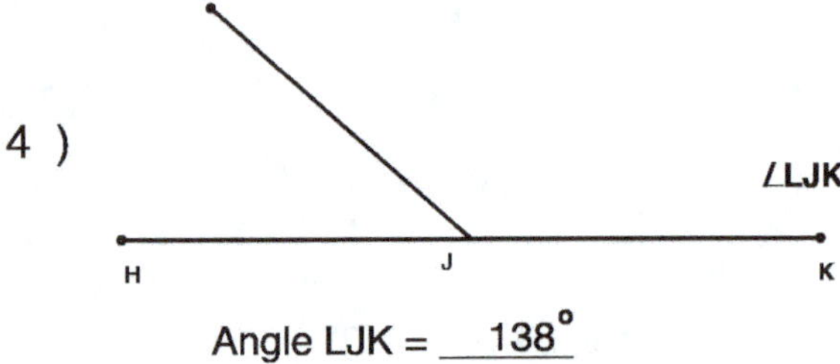

Angle LJK = 138°

5)

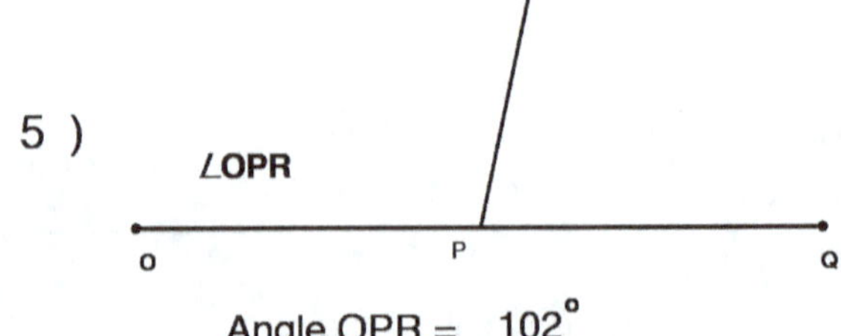

Angle OPR = 102°

6)

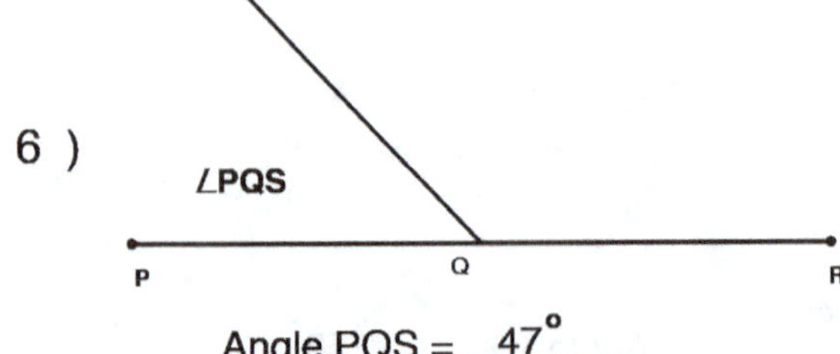

Angle PQS = 47°

EXERCISE 3

1)

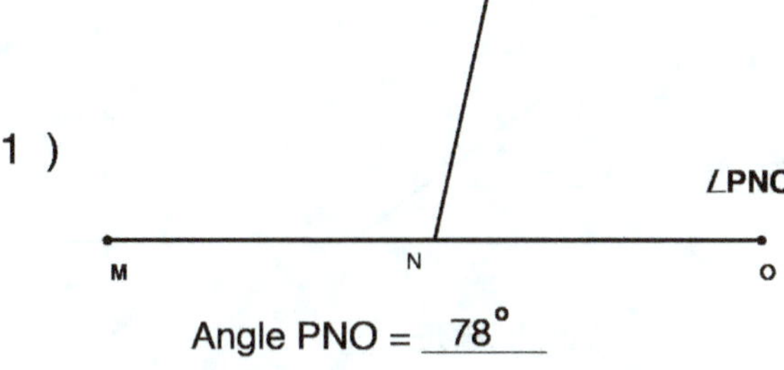

2)

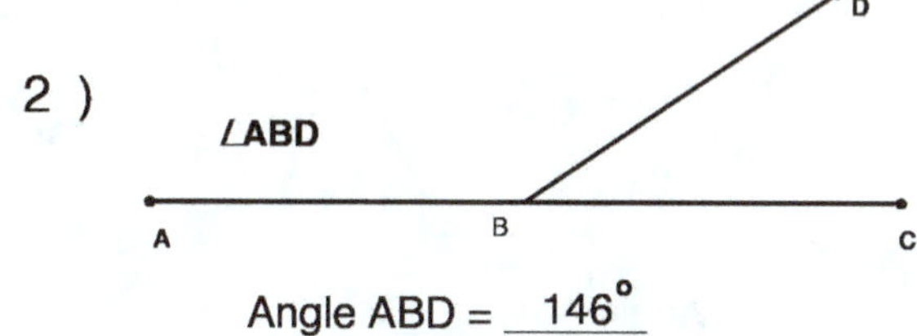

3)

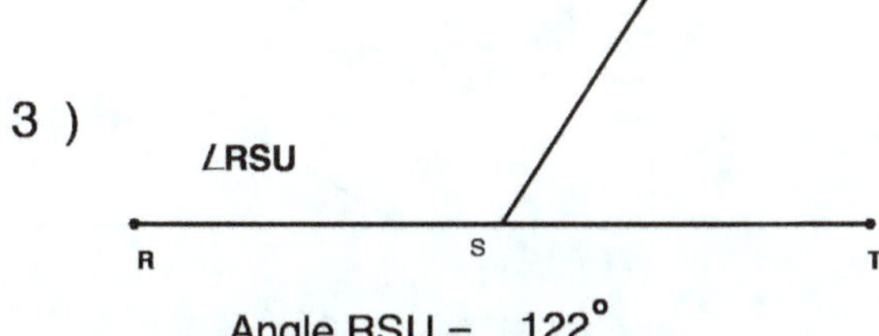

4)

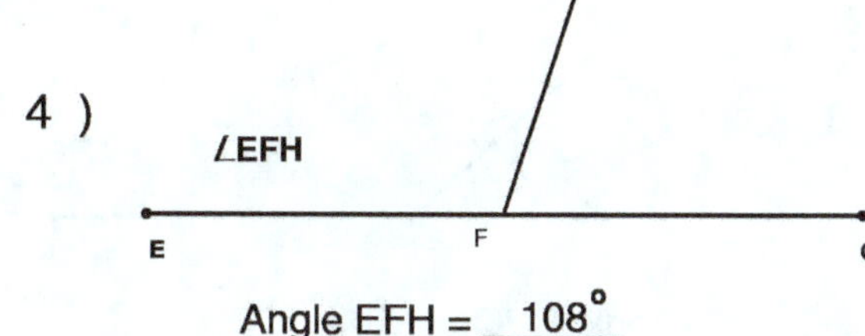

5)

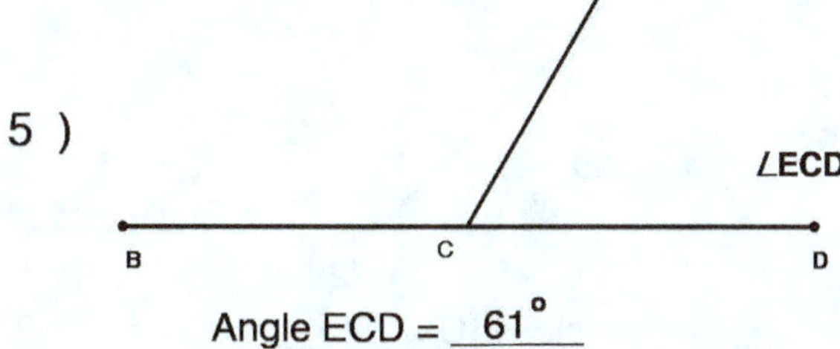

6)

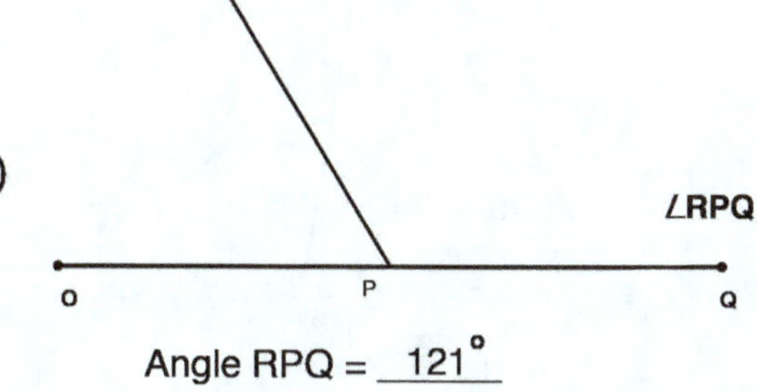

EXERCISE 4

1)

Angle JGH = 62°

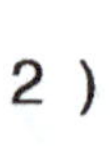

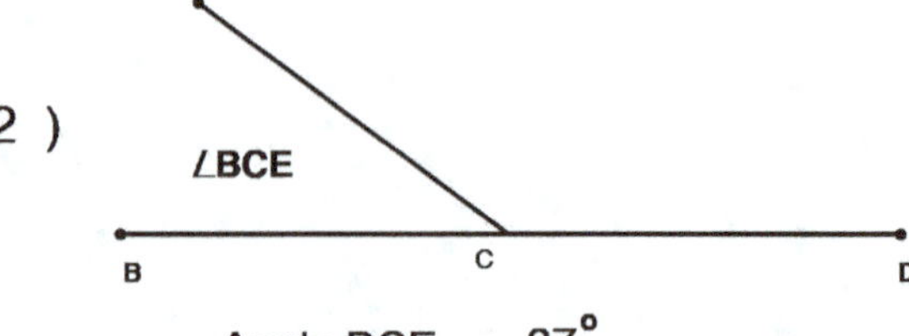

Angle BCE = 37°

3)

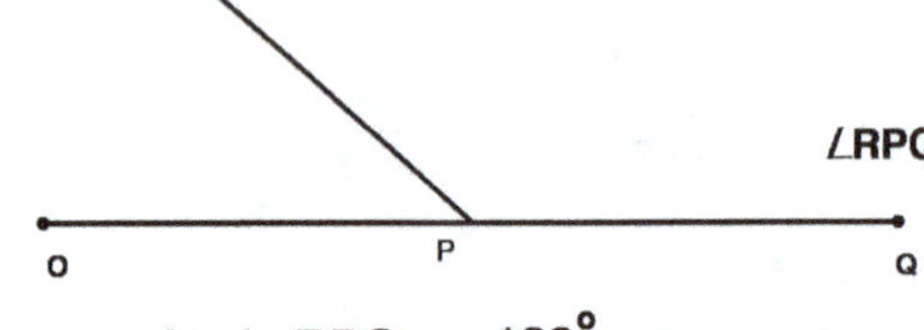

Angle RPQ = 138°

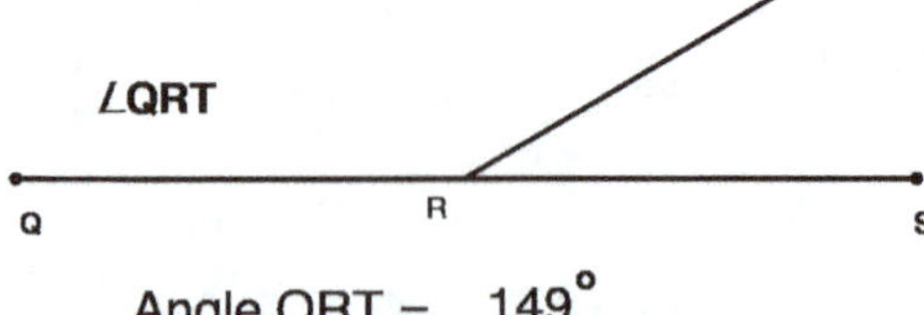

Angle QRT = 149°

5)

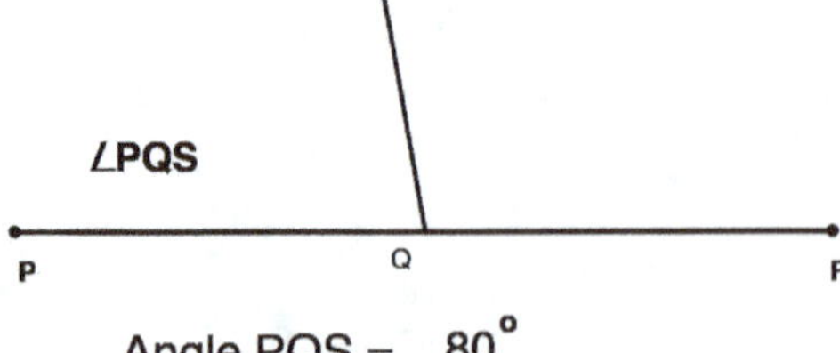

Angle PQS = 80°

6)

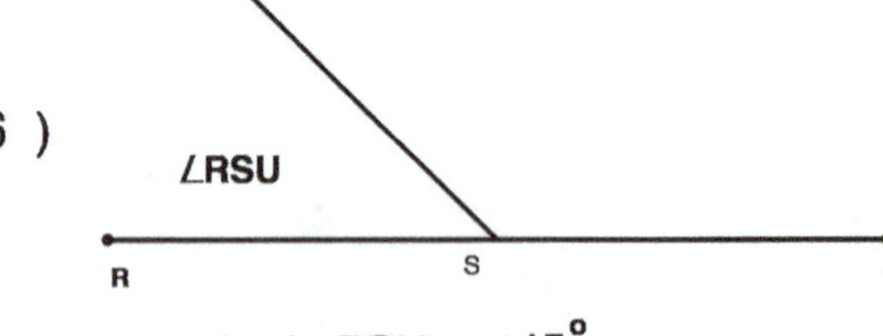

Angle RSU = 45°

EXERCISE 5

1)

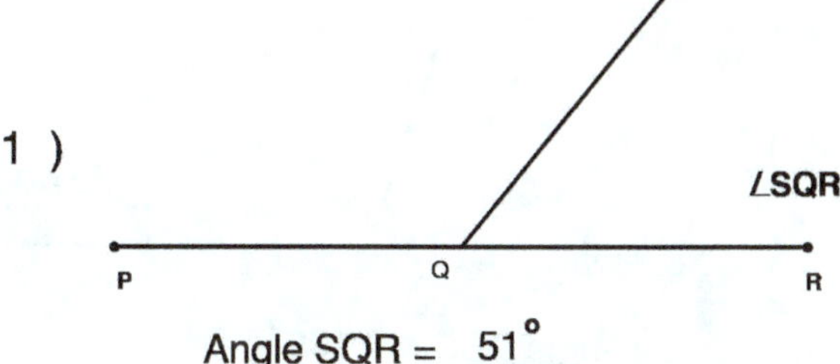

Angle SQR = 51°

2)

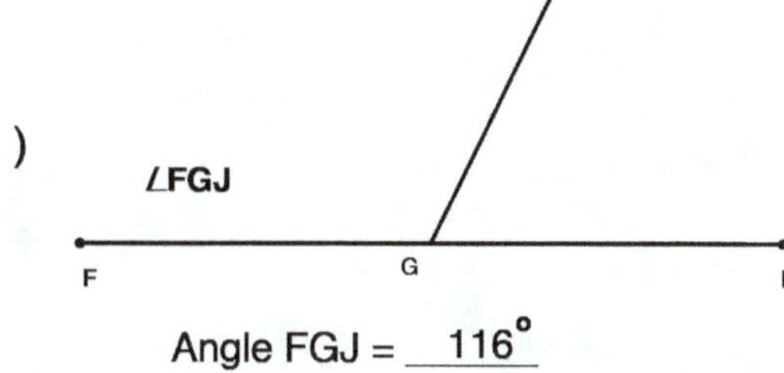

Angle FGJ = 116°

3)

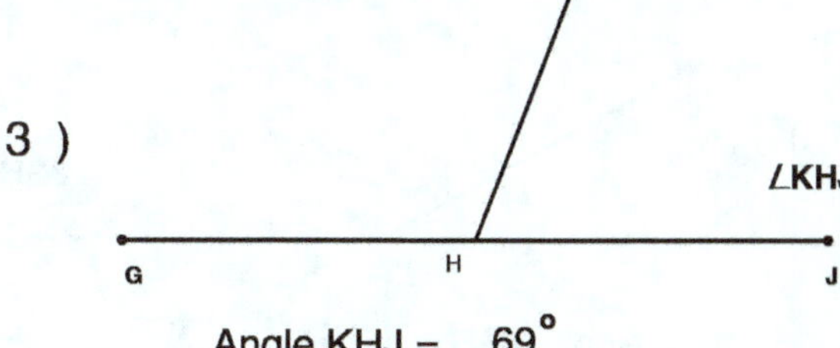

Angle KHJ = 69°

4)

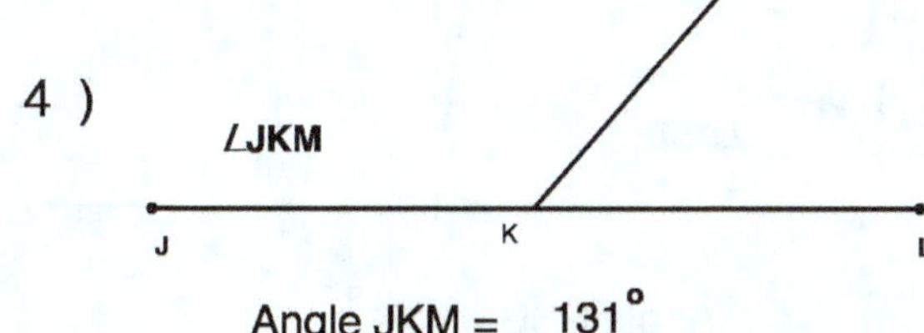

Angle JKM = 131°

5)

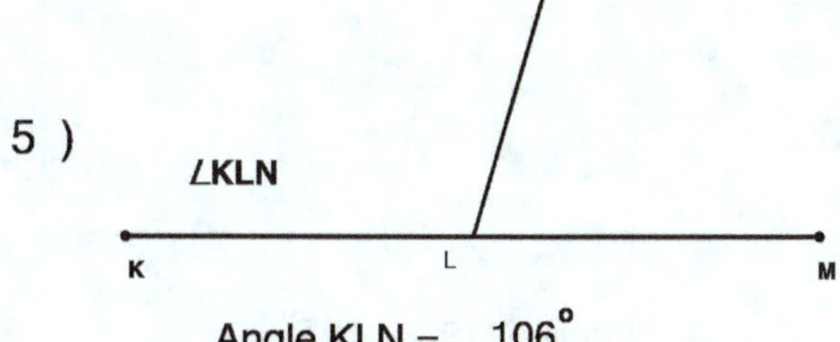

Angle KLN = 106°

6)

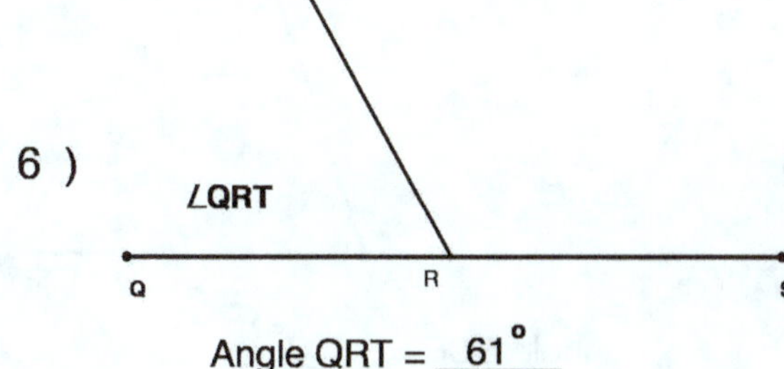

Angle QRT = 61°

EXERCISE 6

1)

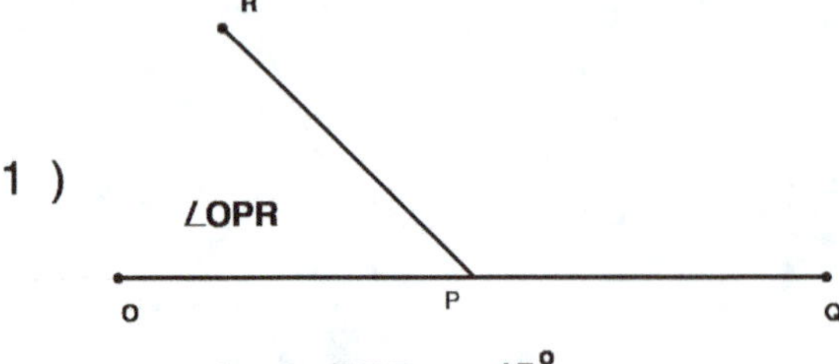

Angle OPR = 45°

2)

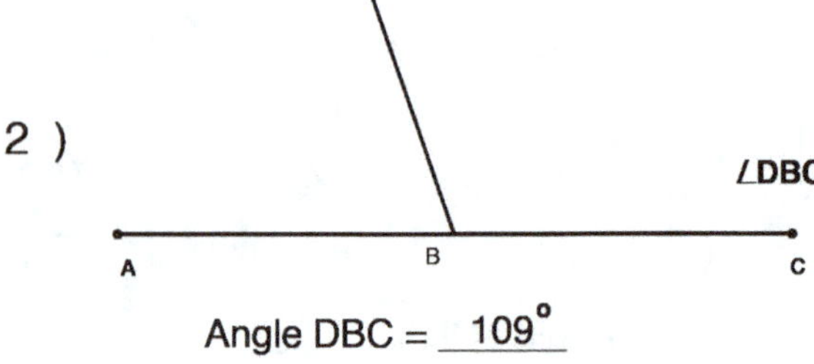

Angle DBC = 109°

3)

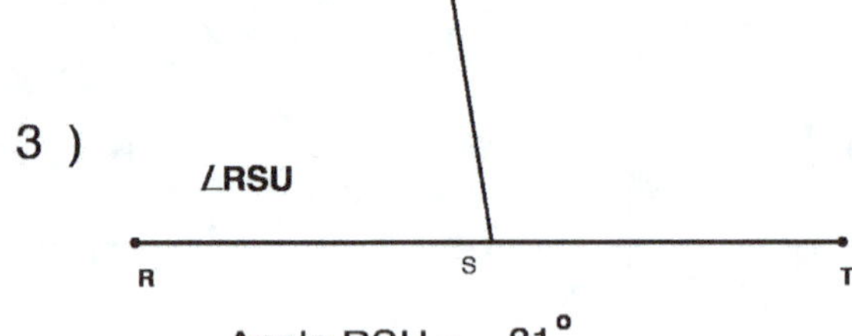

Angle RSU = 81°

4)

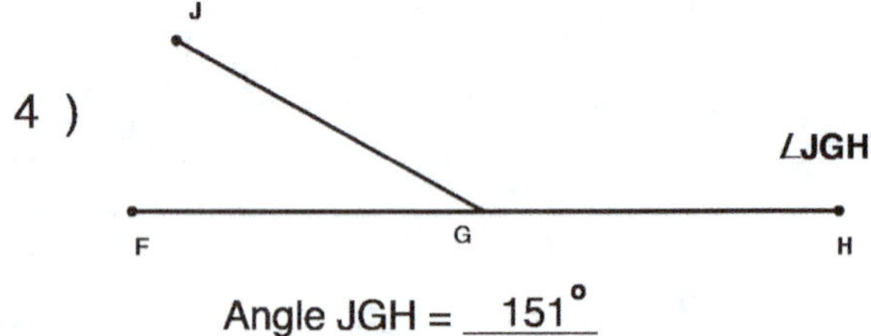

Angle JGH = 151°

5)

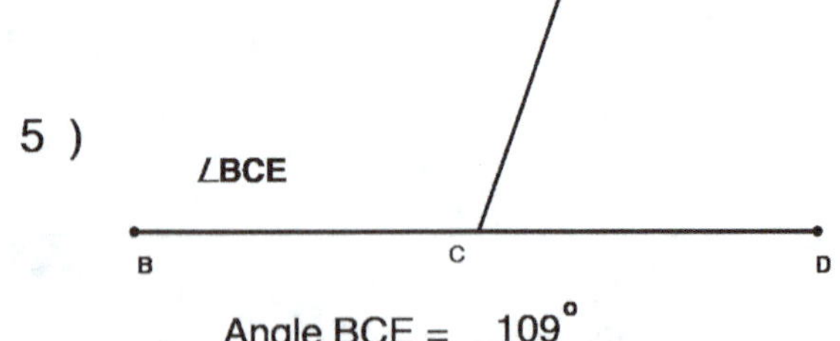

Angle BCE = 109°

6)

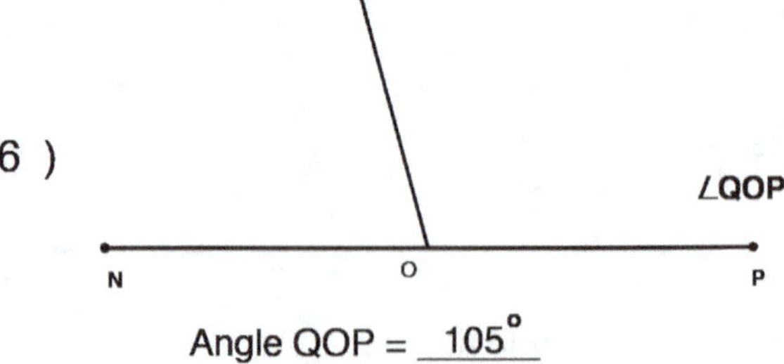

Angle QOP = 105°

EXERCISE
7

1)

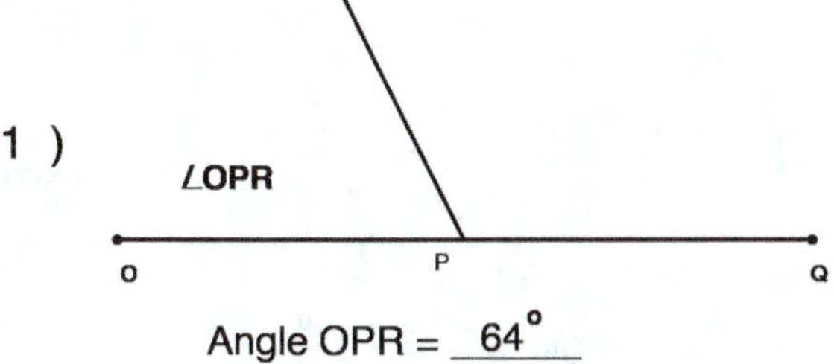

Angle OPR = 64°

2)

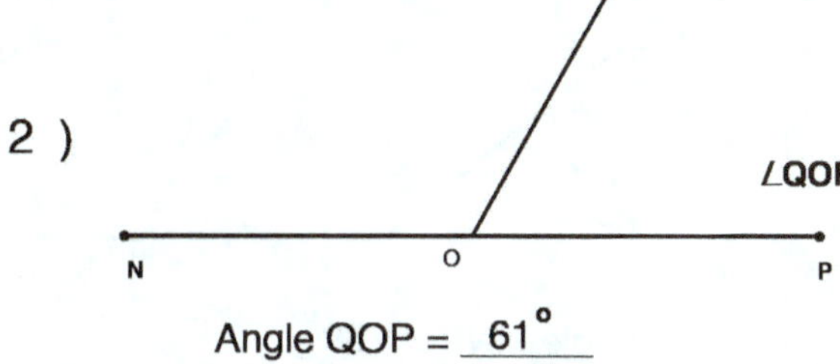

Angle QOP = 61°

3)

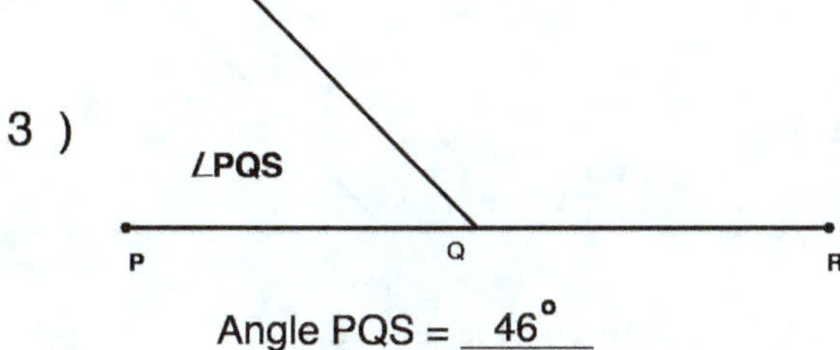

Angle PQS = 46°

4)

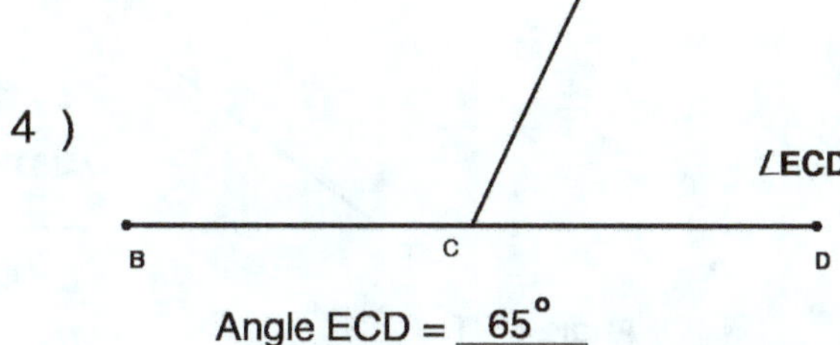

Angle ECD = 65°

5)

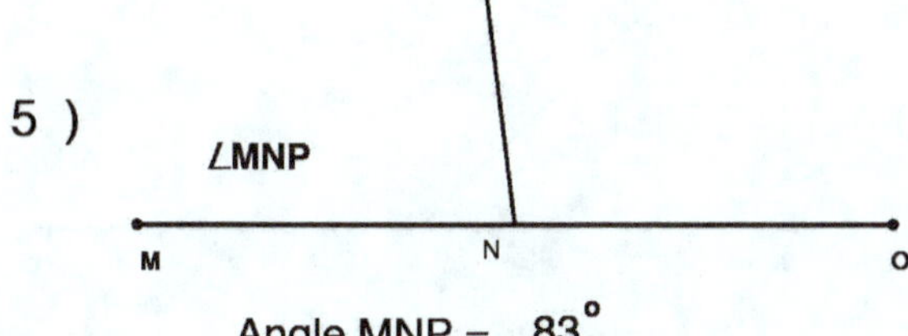

Angle MNP = 83°

6)

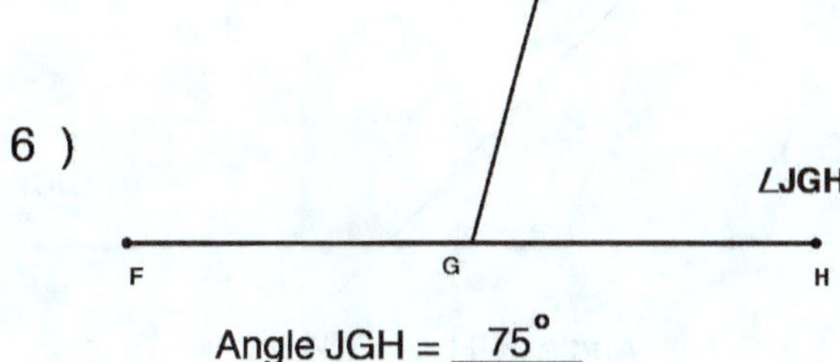

Angle JGH = 75°

EXERCISE 8

1)

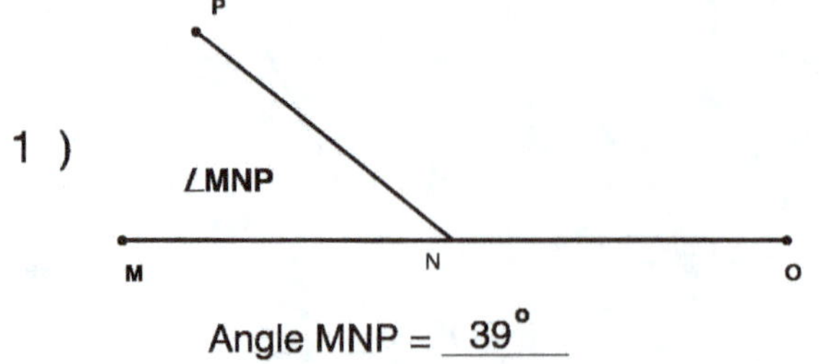

Angle MNP = 39°

2)

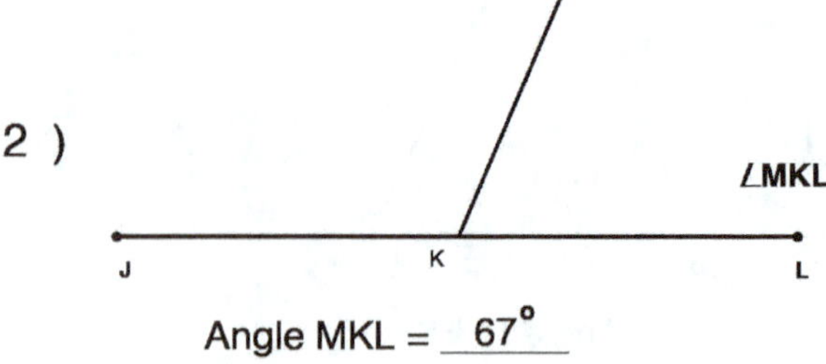

Angle MKL = 67°

3)

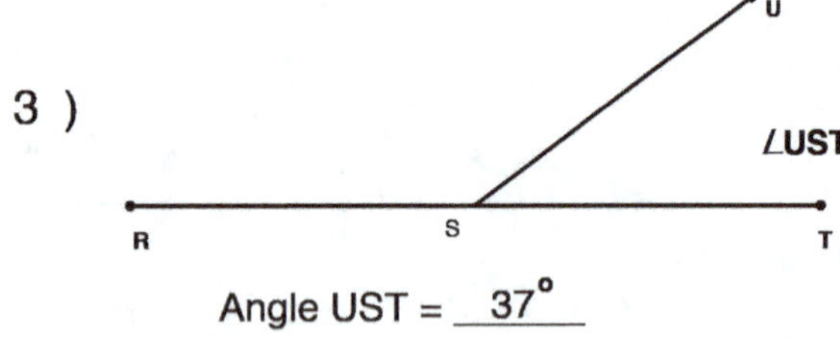

Angle UST = 37°

4)

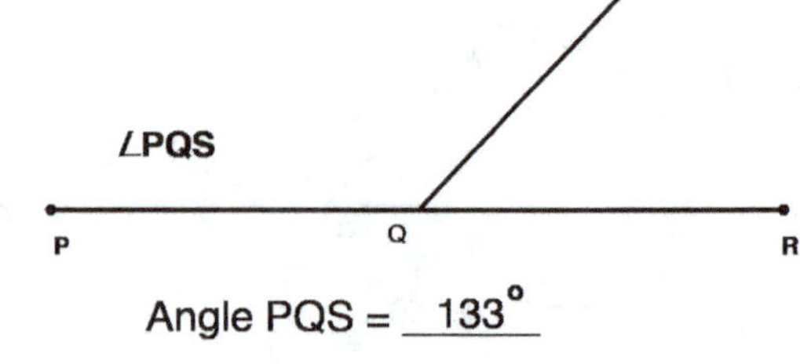

Angle PQS = 133°

5)

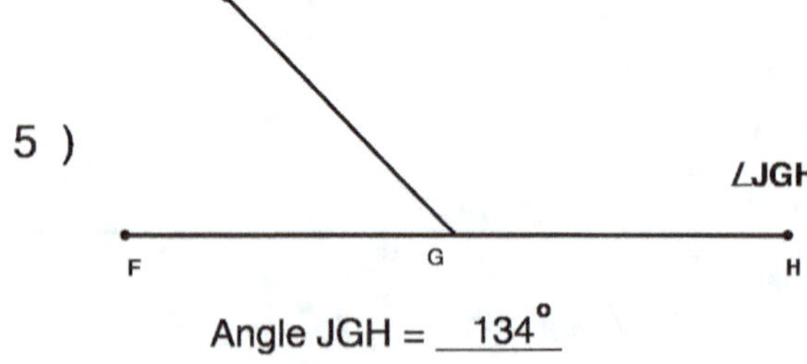

Angle JGH = 134°

6)

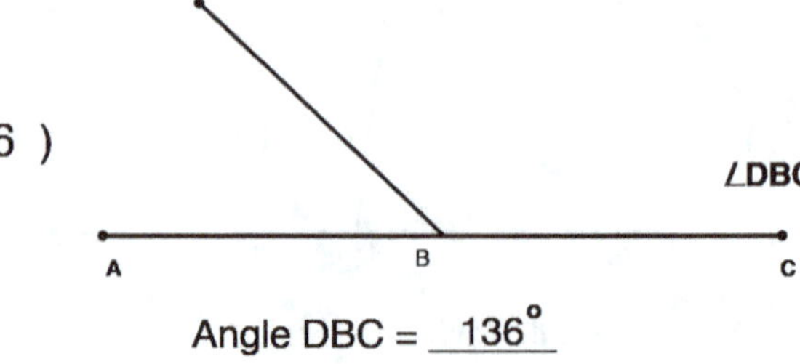

Angle DBC = 136°

EXERCISE 9

1)

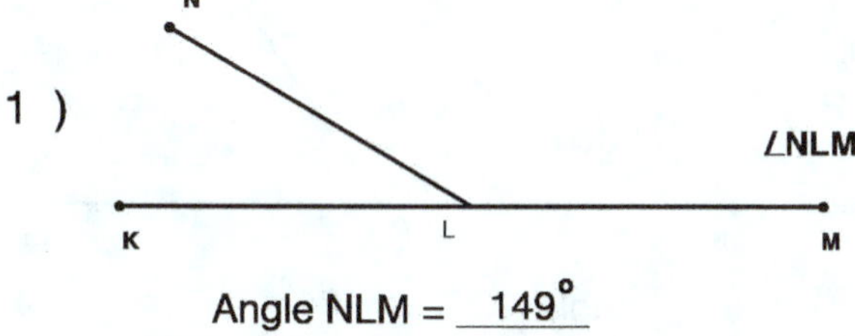

Angle NLM = 149°

2)

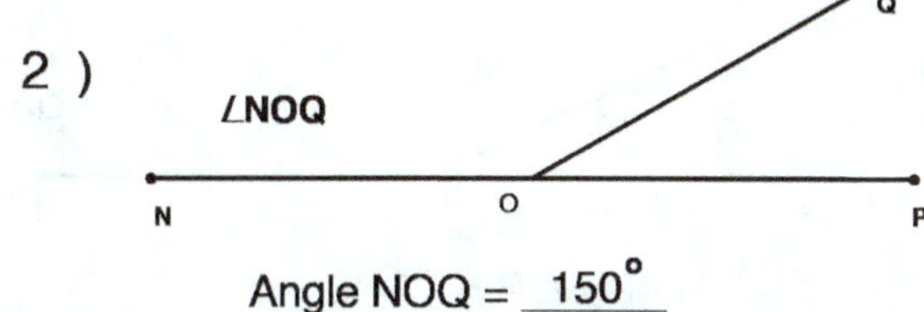

Angle NOQ = 150°

3)

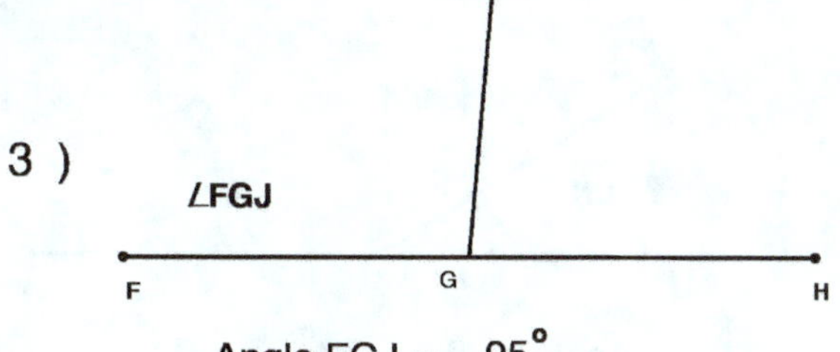

Angle FGJ = 95°

4)

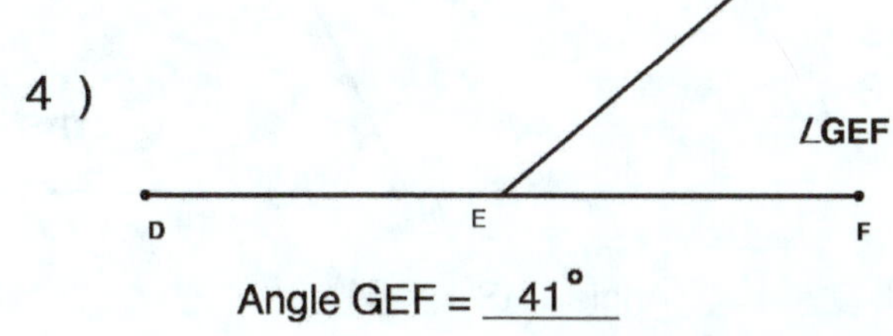

Angle GEF = 41°

5)

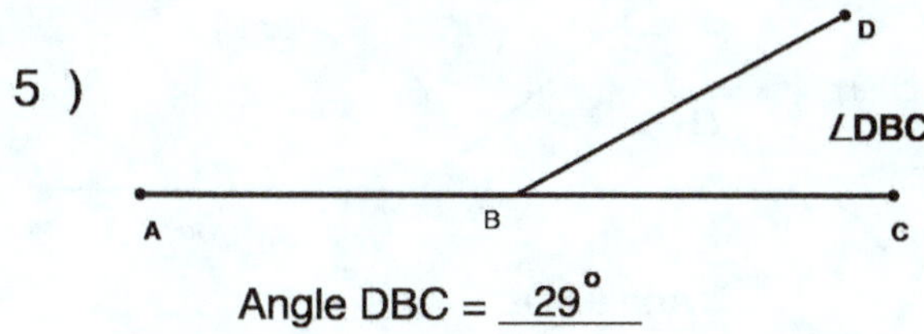

Angle DBC = 29°

6)

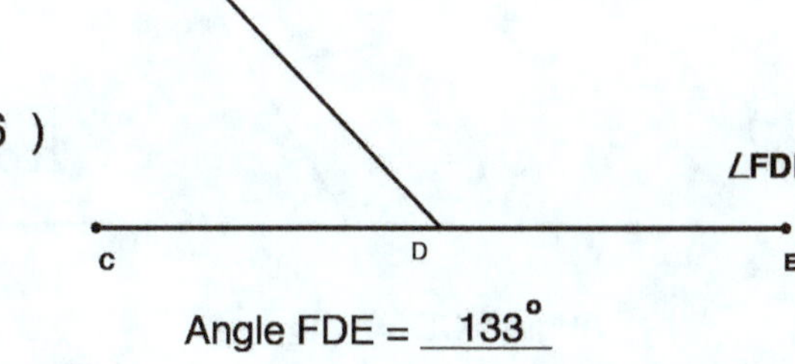

Angle FDE = 133°

EXERCISE 10

1)

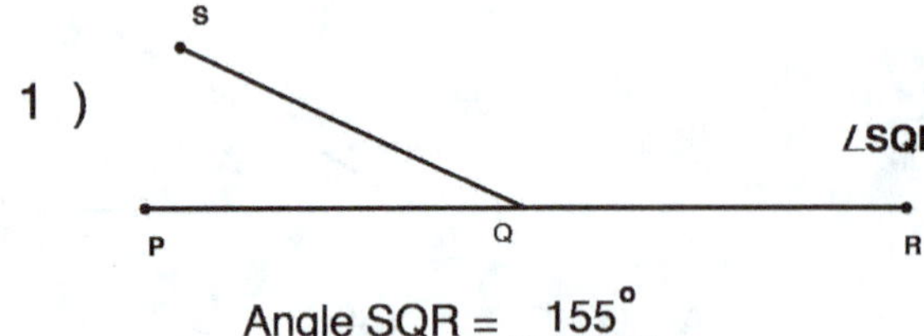

Angle SQR = 155°

2)

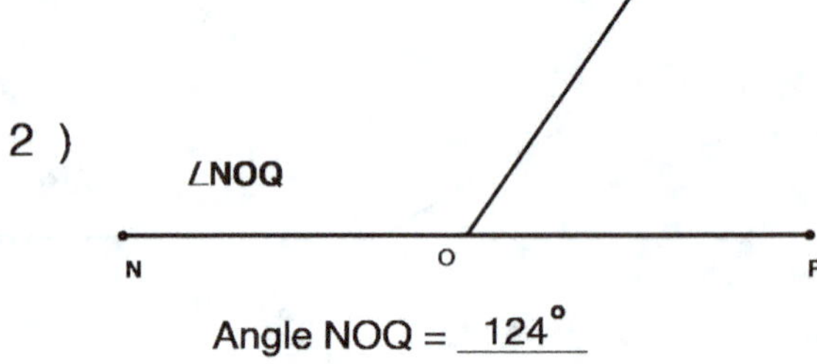

Angle NOQ = 124°

3)

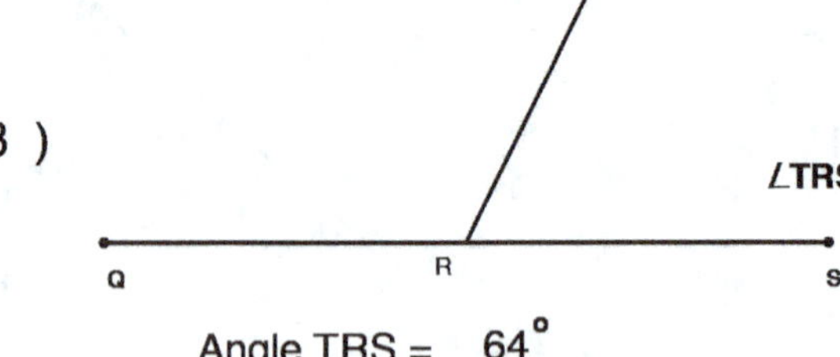

Angle TRS = 64°

4)

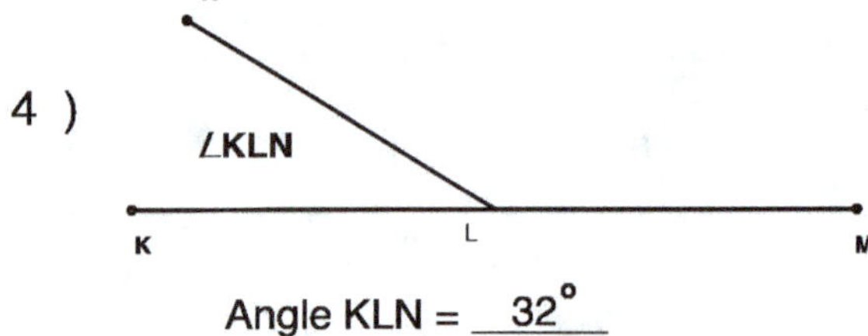

Angle KLN = 32°

5)

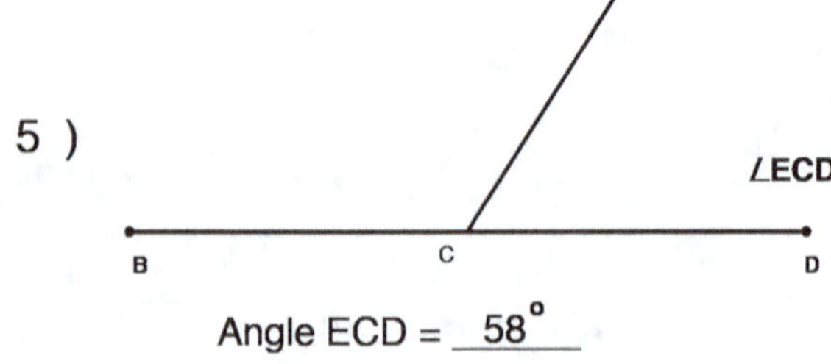

Angle ECD = 58°

6)

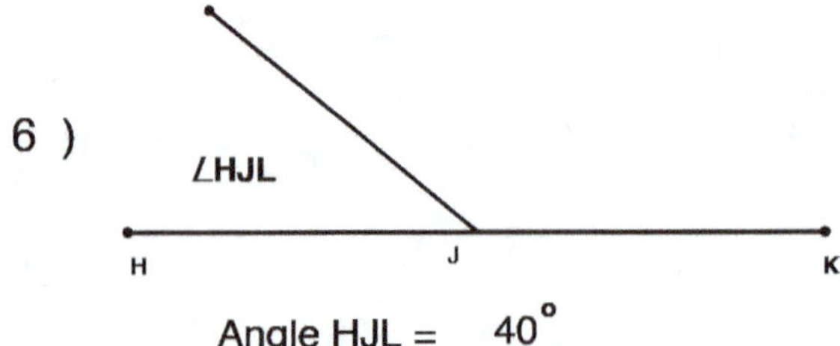

Angle HJL = 40°

EXERCISE 11

1)

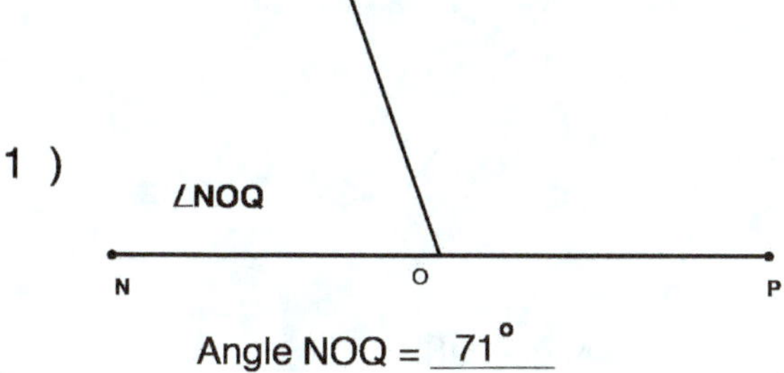

Angle NOQ = 71°

2)

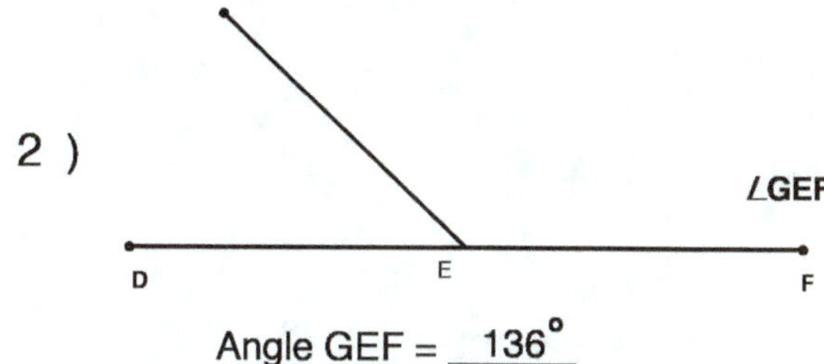

Angle GEF = 136°

3)

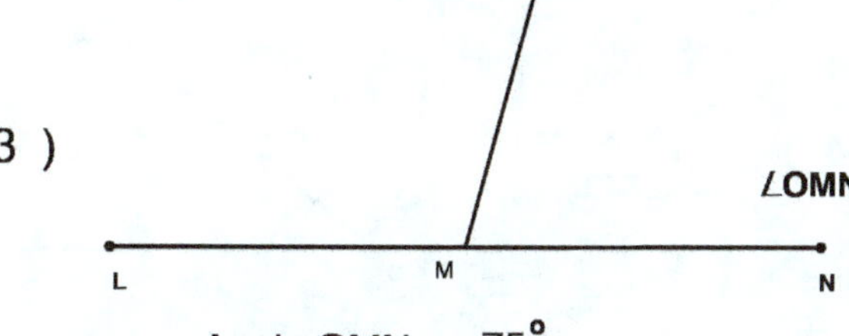

Angle OMN = 75°

4)

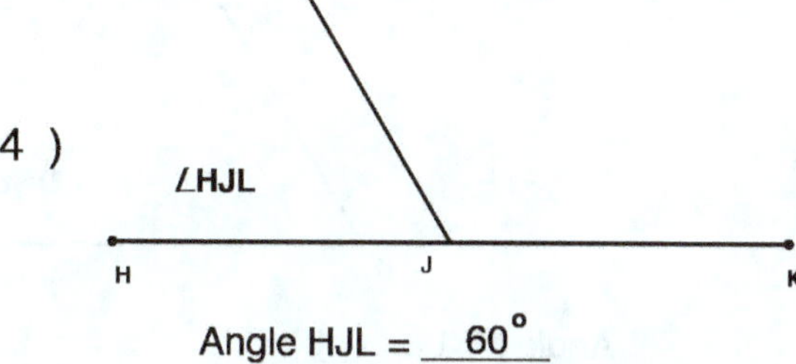

Angle HJL = 60°

5)

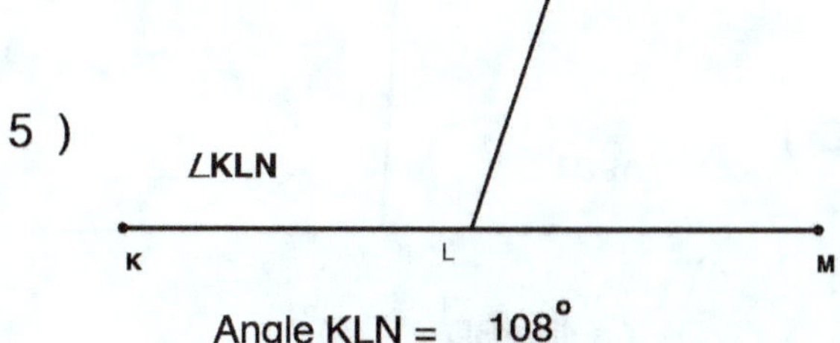

Angle KLN = 108°

6)

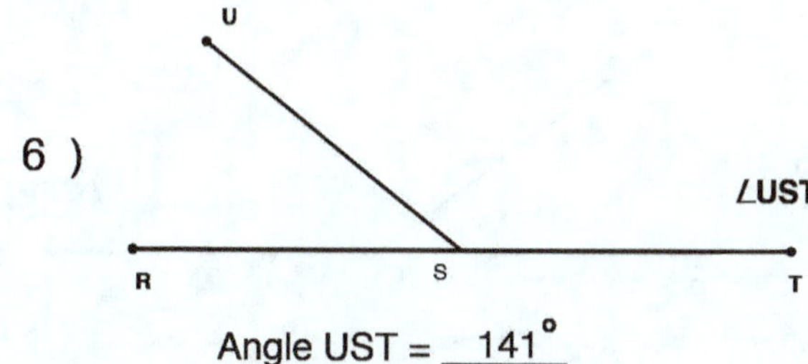

Angle UST = 141°

EXERCISE
12

1)

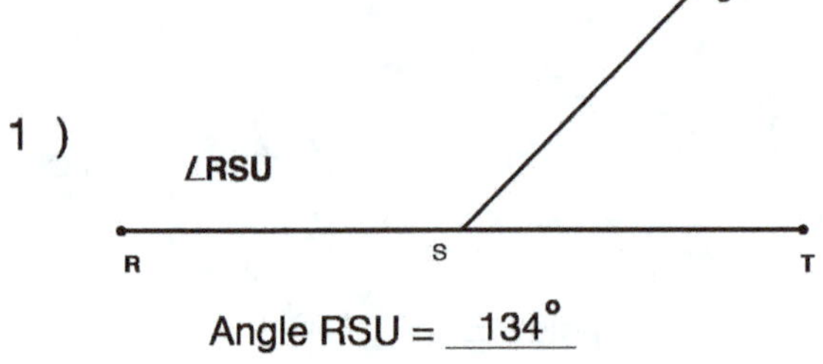

Angle RSU = 134°

2)

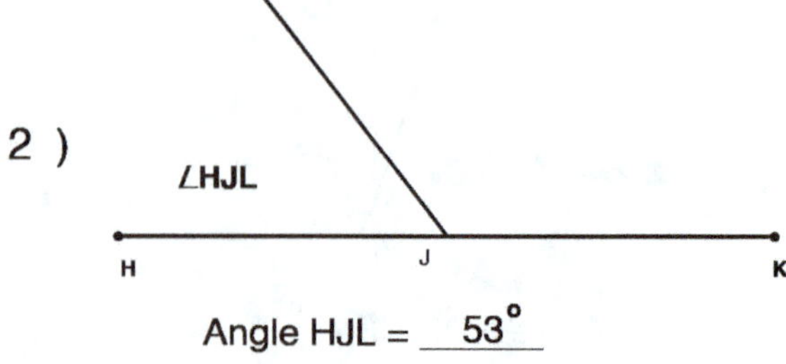

Angle HJL = 53°

3)

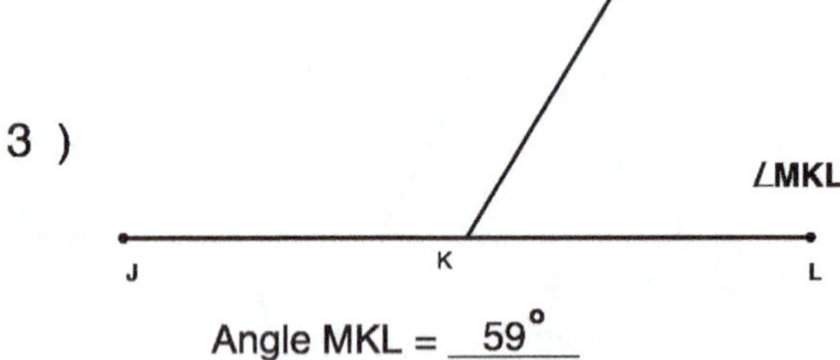

Angle MKL = 59°

4)

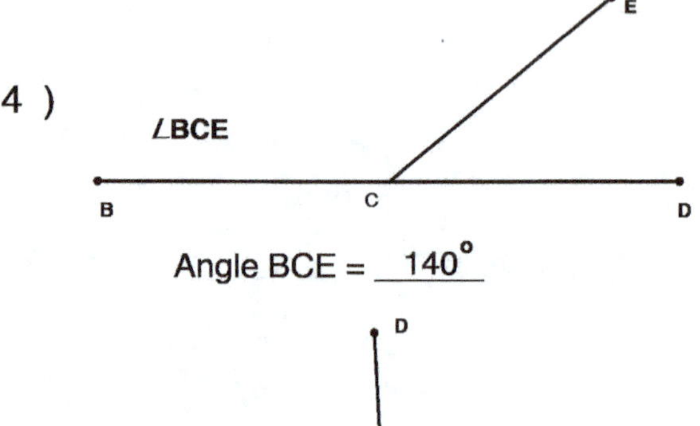

Angle BCE = 140°

5)

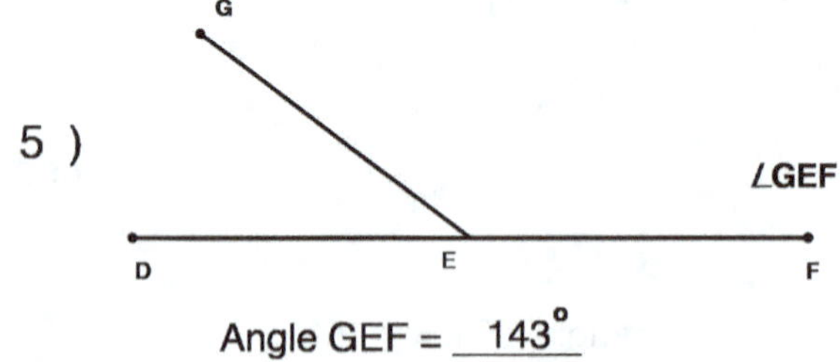

Angle GEF = 143°

6)

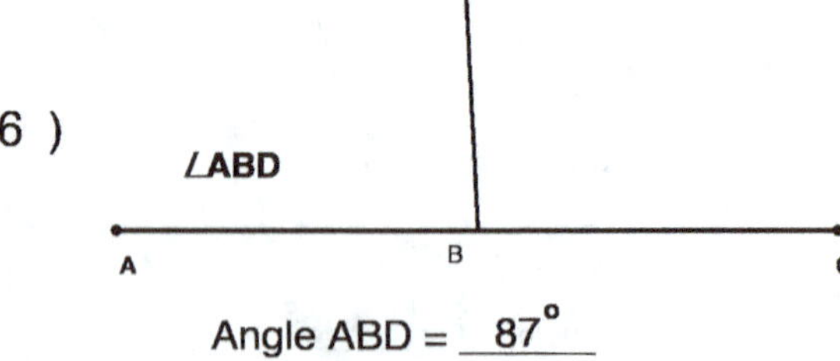

Angle ABD = 87°

EXERCISE 13

1)

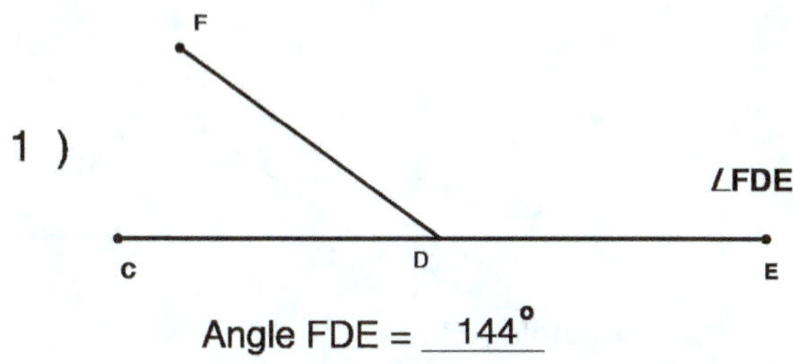

Angle FDE = 144°

2)

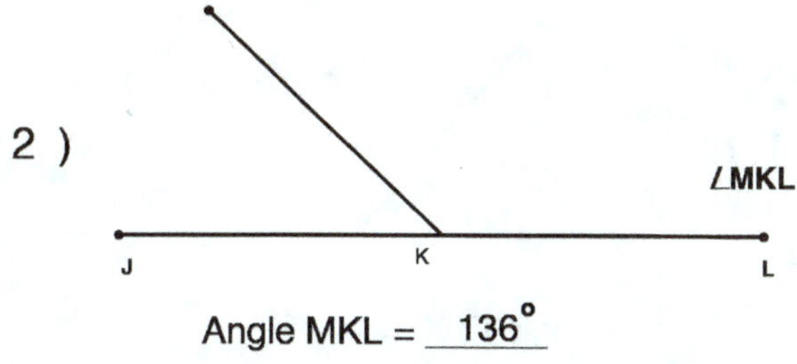

Angle MKL = 136°

3)

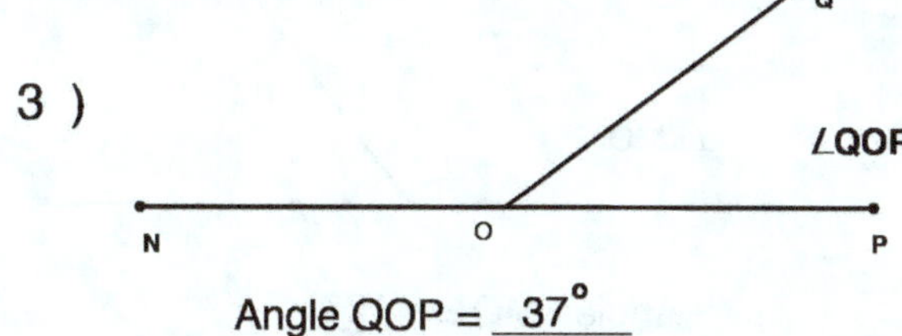

Angle QOP = 37°

4)

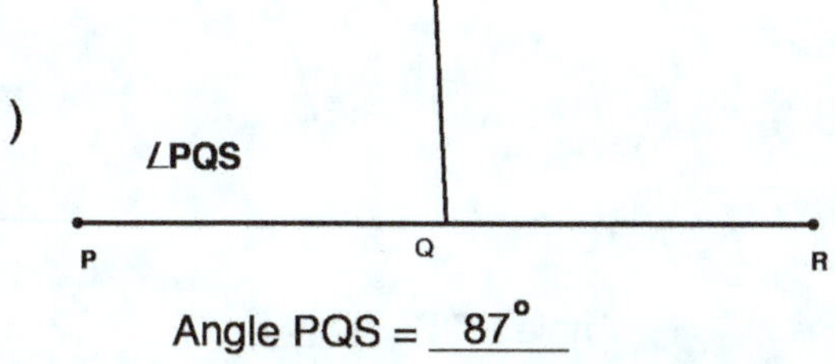

Angle PQS = 87°

5)

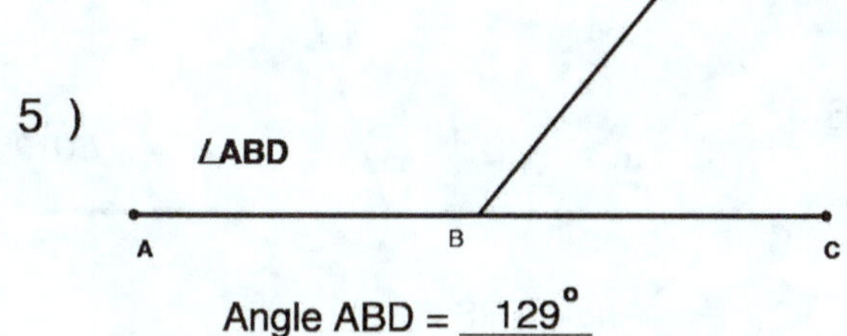

Angle ABD = 129°

6)

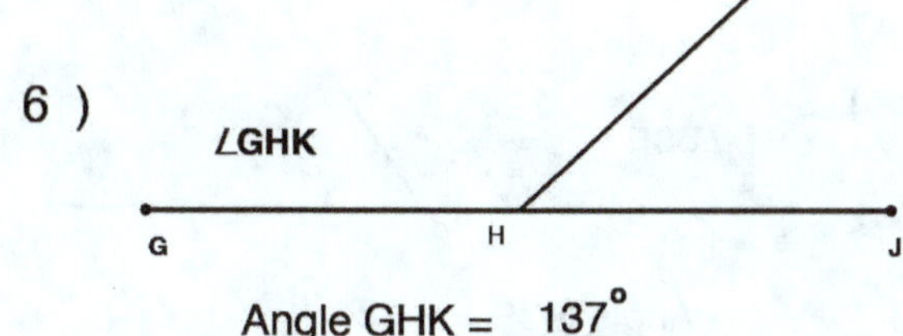

Angle GHK = 137°

EXERCISE 14

1)

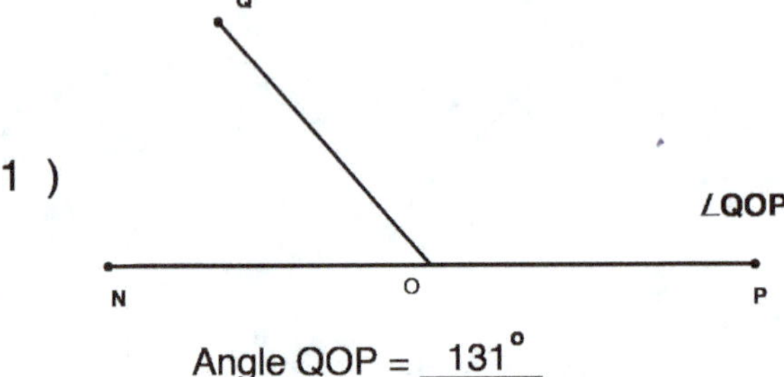

Angle QOP = 131°

2)

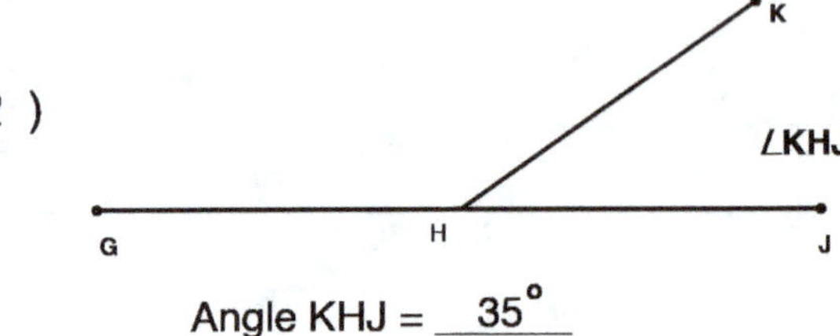

Angle KHJ = 35°

3)

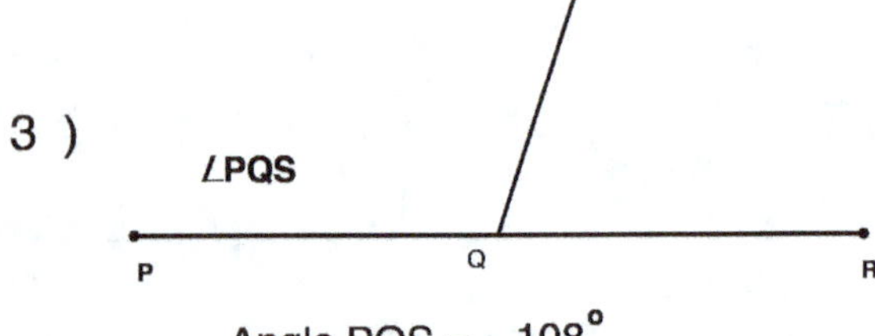

Angle PQS = 108°

4)

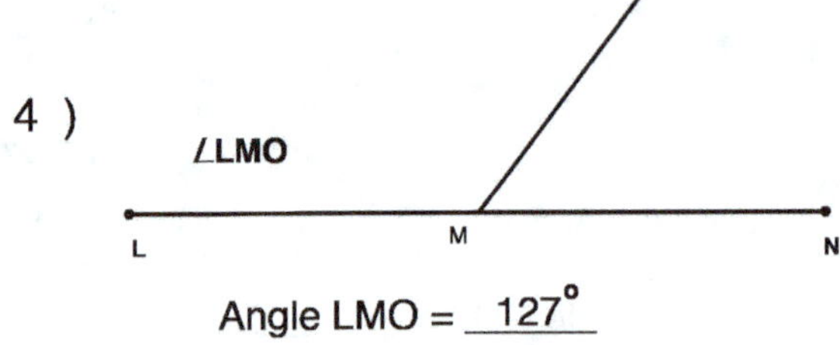

Angle LMO = 127°

5)

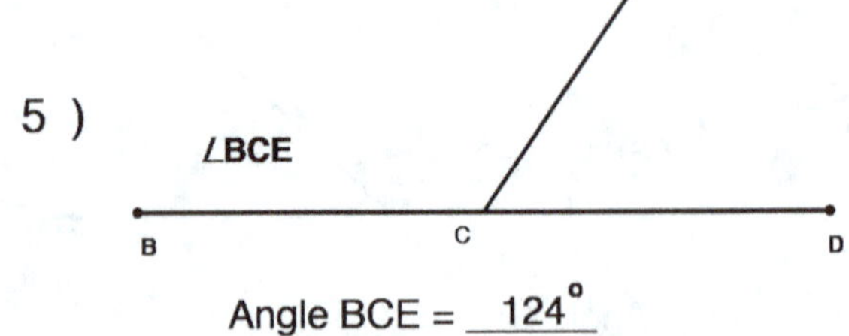

Angle BCE = 124°

6)

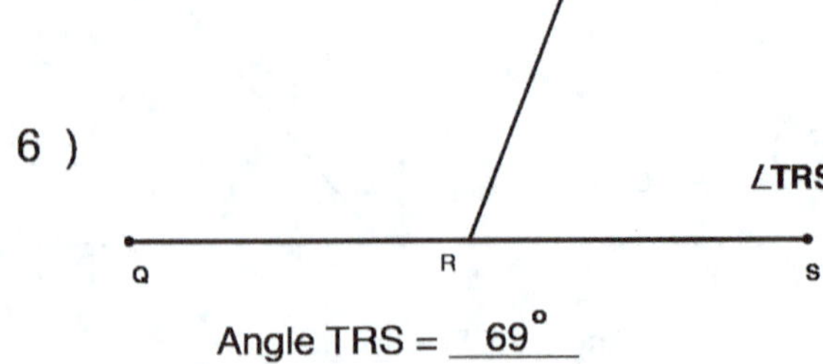

Angle TRS = 69°

EXERCISE 15

1)

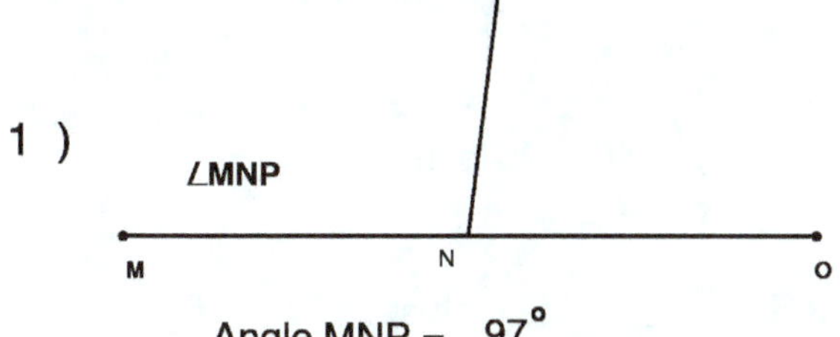

Angle MNP = 97°

2)

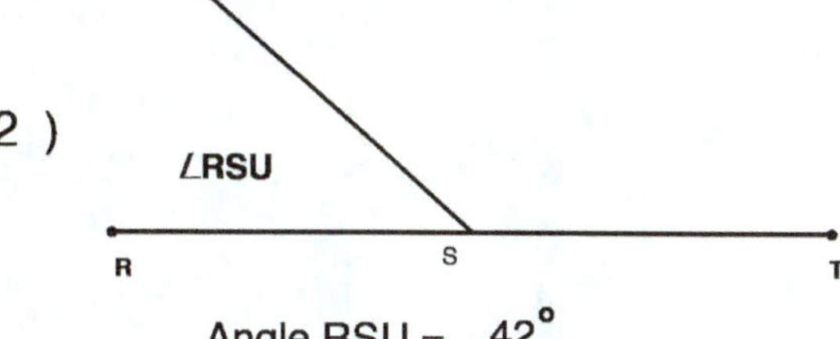

Angle RSU = 42°

3)

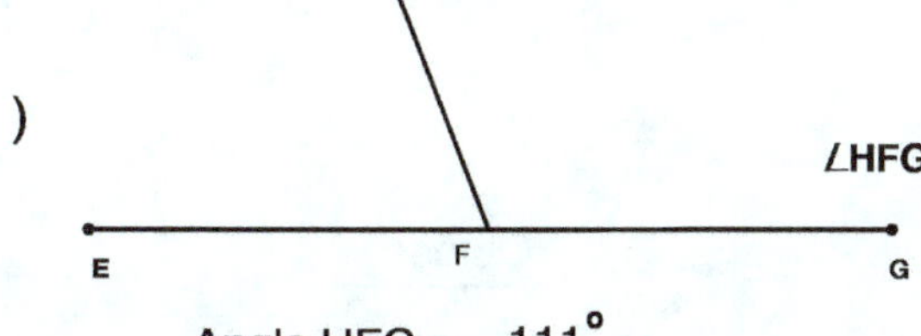

Angle HFG = 111°

4)

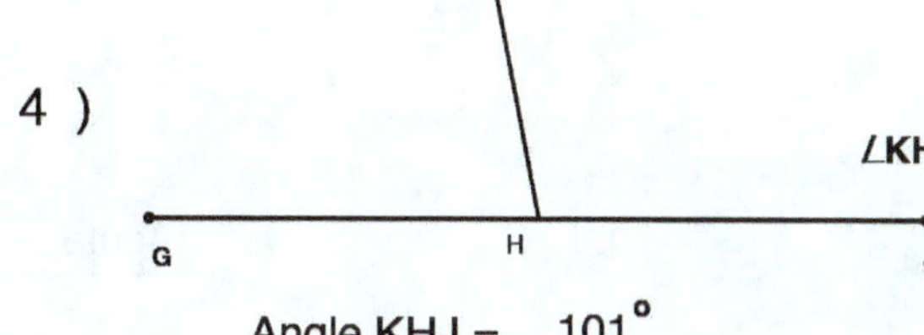

Angle KHJ = 101°

5)

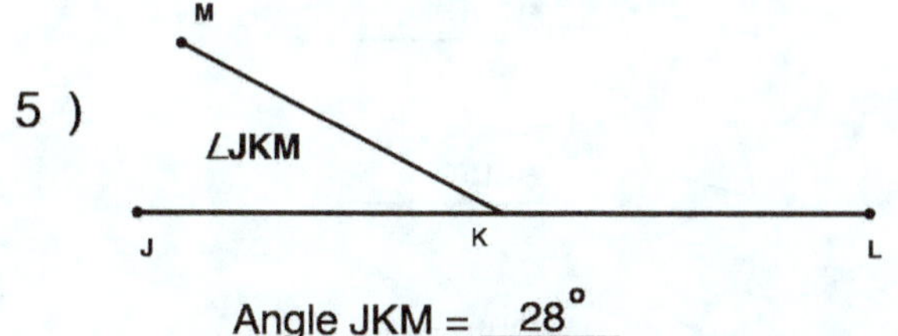

Angle JKM = 28°

6)

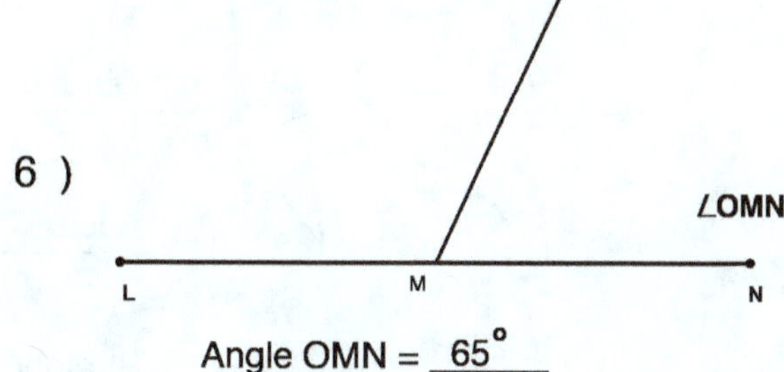

Angle OMN = 65°

Angle Classification

Exercise 1

1) Acute

2) Obtuse

3) Obtuse

4) Acute

5) Acute

6) Obtuse

7) Straight

8) Acute

9) Obtuse

10) Right

Exercise 2

1) Acute

2)  Right

3)  Obtuse

4)  Acute

5)  Straight

6) Obtuse

7) Obtuse

8)  Acute

9)  Acute

10)  Obtuse

Angle Classification

EXERCISE 3

1) Straight
2) Obtuse
3) Obtuse
4) Right
5) Acute
6) Acute
7) Acute
8) Acute
9) Obtuse
10) Obtuse

EXERCISE 4

1) Obtuse
2) Acute
3) Acute
4) Obtuse
5)  Acute
6) Acute
7) Obtuse
8) Straight
9) Obtuse
10) Right

Angle Classification

Exercise 5

1) Obtuse

2) Straight

3) Acute

4) Obtuse

5) Obtuse

6) Right

7) Acute

8) Acute

9) Obtuse

10) Acute

Exercise 6

1) Acute

2) Obtuse

3) Acute

4) Obtuse

5)  Straight

6) Obtuse

7) Acute

8) Acute

9) Right

10)  Obtuse

ANGLE CLASSIFICATION

EXERCISE 7

1)	 Right	6)	 Straight
2)	 Acute	7)	 Obtuse
3)	 Obtuse	8)	 Obtuse
4)	 Acute	9)	Obtuse
5)	 Acute	10)	 Acute

EXERCISE 8

1)	 Straight	6)	 Acute
2)	 Obtuse	7)	 Acute
3)	 Obtuse	8)	 Right
4)	 Obtuse	9)	 Acute
5)	 Acute	10)	Obtuse

ANGLE CLASSIFICATION

EXERCISE 9

1)  Acute
2)  Obtuse
3)  Acute
4)  Obtuse
5)  Obtuse
6)  Right
7)  Acute
8)  Obtuse
9)  Acute
10)  Straight

EXERCISE 10

1)  Right
2)  Acute
3)  Obtuse
4)  Straight
5)  Obtuse
6)  Acute
7)  Obtuse
8)  Obtuse
9)  Acute
10)  Acute

ANGLE CLASSIFICATION

1. 143° = obtuse
2. 111° = obtuse
3. 10° = acute
4. 102° = obtuse
5. 74° = acute
6. 124° = obtuse
7. 116° = obtuse
8. 126° = obtuse
9. 158° = obtuse
10. 39° = acute
11. 77° = acute
12. 31° = acute
13. 133° = obtuse
14. 113° = obtuse
15. 34° = acute
16. 127° = obtuse
17. 139° = obtuse
18. 174° = obtuse
19. 84° = acute
20. 165° = obtuse

www.ingramcontent.com/pod-product-compliance
Lightning Source LLC
LaVergne TN
LVHW060627170826
845677LV00027B/1628

* 9 7 9 8 8 6 9 4 4 4 4 6 2 *